P MS TO A T

THE WINNING FORMULA FOR WRITING NONFICTION SHORT STORIES THAT SELL

By B.J. Taylor

Cover illustration by C. W. Walker
Cover and Interior Design by Steven W. Booth,
        www.GeniusBookServices.com

Contact B.J.:
      bj@bjtaylor.com
      www.bjtaylor.com
      www.bjtaylorblog.wordpress.com

What Writers Say About the Formula

"I went to your session on writing short stories that sell. Well, it worked! I will be published in *Chicken Soup for the Soul: Multitasking Mom's Survival Guide*. Soooo excited. Thanks for teaching me your formula. The publication of my story is encouragement to the max."

— Gwyn

"You're a natural teacher and encourager and you've put it into an easy to understand formula that you so brilliantly teach. YES, you should put it into a book."

— Julie

"I think your formula is fantastic. It has helped many people get into print."

— Kay

"That's your story, Christie." I can still hear B.J.'s encouraging words from our time together at a writers conference. She was right, because thanks to her *Guideposts* selected me as a 2014 workshopper. I applied her winning formula which made the writing process more manageable and allowed me to write with depth and focus. I gained so much invaluable wisdom and gleaned practical insight from her teaching. I'm proof that her tips and formula really do work!"

— Christie

"I was so impressed at how easy you made writing inspirational short stories with your P MS to a T formula."

— Wanda

"This formula worked so well for me that I was able to use it to write a story that was accepted by *Chicken Soup for the Soul: Hope and Miracles.*"

— Judee

"I attended B.J.'s class in 2011 and learned the P MS to a T formula, then submitted a story for publication. It didn't get picked, but I didn't give up. I submitted again and in the next 18 months had eight stories accepted and printed in *Chicken Soup for the Soul* books. I'm a published author! Thanks, B.J., for sharing your formula."

— Lynn

"I met B.J. at the writers' conference in Florida, attended her sessions, and submitted stories to the *Guideposts* contest. I didn't win, but they liked one of my stories and it will appear in *Angels on Earth*. I'm just as thrilled as if I won!"

— Carin

This book is dedicated to all writers who are determined to become published, prolific authors.

Whether you already know the formula and are using it, or you are hearing about it for the first time, it is my hope you will find what you need in these pages to help you write succinct, inspirational, personal experience short stories that move and entertain the reader.

I stand up and cheer for those of you who have attended my workshop classes and have gone on to use this formula to craft stories that have been accepted for publication. I applaud your effort and determination.

If you are already a published author, would you like to be more prolific? And if you have not been published yet, are you dreaming about it? If you believe, work hard, and never give up, you can make your dream a reality.

Dream big but start small.

CONTENTS

CHAPTER 1

Dream Big but Start Small

It's a good thing we have more time together than an hour-long workshop at a writers conference. I have so much to share with you.

Let's get started by talking about why we should dream big but start small.

Do you have an idea for a novel? Maybe two or three? Maybe you've written a novel but it hasn't been published yet.

Have you thought of writing a nonfiction book based on a life experience?

Those are all grand goals. We should have big hopes and big dreams. But I encourage you to think about getting publication credits under your belt. I'm not saying you have to exclusively do one or the other. You can work on your novel and write short stories at the same time. Plan to do both.

Here's why.

Have you heard the word "platform" before?

It's that dreaded "P" word agents and publishers talk about. It's the thing the marketing department at a publishing house wants to know first and foremost when considering a book for publication. What is the author's platform? And a platform can encompass many things, including: Where has the author been published? What kind of social media does the author have? Is the author on Twitter, Facebook, LinkedIn, or other locations? Does the author have a website? A blog? A newsletter?

All of these things contribute to an author's platform. It's enough to scare the dickens out of you when you hear it at conferences. But it doesn't have to. Social media is important today. Everyone is talking about it. If you don't do Twitter, learn how, if you aren't on Facebook, get on it, but don't let either one eclipse your life.

When I first began using social media, I let it consume me. I checked my accounts constantly for fear I'd miss a Tweet or a Facebook comment. Now I have a healthy respect for all of my online connections, including LinkedIn, and I monitor, but don't obsess. It's a fine line. I learned to find balance for the sake of my sanity.

In addition to the need for social media presence is the need for publication credits. What better way to show an editor or agent you have the moxie to make a go of it as a published author? When you submit a story for publication, you must work with an editor to make it just right for their print or online purpose. They may ask for revisions, or an extensive rewrite. They may make changes that don't totally excite you. Learn to be flexible and to allow revisions when necessary.

Become a writer an editor likes to work with. Here's a secret: if you learn to be a good writer (using this winning formula for your short, inspirational stories) your work will be considered of high quality and less likely to be edited. I've found that to be true in many instances. Granted, there are many publications that heavily edit no matter what, but as an experienced writer with a strong sense of self, you can accept that the finished product is what the publication needs and agree to the changes if they are not morally or ethically against your character. If the story gets out there in print, even if it isn't your exact word-for-word piece, isn't that the ultimate goal?

So that's a long explanation of why you should DREAM BIG but start small.

Personal experience short stories published in numerous places will carry a lot of weight in both editors' and agents' eyes as they look at your writing career as a whole.

CHAPTER 2

What's a Nonfiction Short Story?

A nonfiction short story is a work of truth. It's about personal experience and the subject matter is factual. The writer of nonfiction writes about actual people, places, and things.

The word "nonfiction" is important because if you look up "short story" you will find the following definition: A short story is a short work of fiction usually dealing with few characters.

Let's get something straight. What we're talking about in this book is a TRUE, real life, personal experience story. A true story is still a story. And for our purposes, it is short. I call it short because the markets for these types of stories are usually 1,000 to 1,500 words.

Many of the elements of "short story" pertain to both fiction and nonfiction.

Consider this from Concise Encyclopedia:

"A short story usually presents a single significant episode or scene involving a limited number of characters. The form encourages economy of setting and concise narration; character is disclosed in action and dramatic encounter but seldom fully developed. A short story may concentrate on the creation of mood."

CliffsNotes adds:

"Because of the shorter length, a short story usually focuses on one plot, one main character (with a few additional minor characters), and one central theme."

And from Short Story: Thematic Elements:

"In a short story, a character usually experiences some kind of change. Most or all of the story—beginning, middle, and end—revolves around this change. Short stories do not contain an overabundance of characters or deviations from a central plot or theme. They give readers something focused to think about."

Those explanations are exactly what we are going for, but did all of that confuse you? Don't let it. For our purposes, we are discussing a STORY that is short, but that is also TRUE. Therefore, it is a NONFICTION SHORT STORY.

What's NONFICTION?

The elements of nonfiction are characters, plot, and setting. These elements are real, not fabricated. The main character is called the subject. The subject's words, thoughts, and actions are presented in a story. And for our purposes, we are writing a personal recollection, or personal experience, about our own lives that concentrates on one event. We try to recreate stories from memories as accurately as possible. But is it possible to recall the *exact* words spoken years ago during a conversation? Is it possible to remember the *actual* date it happened or even what we were wearing or the street we were on or the restaurant we were in?

You, the writer, are allowed to recall the incident as best you can and to write the story from your memories as you remember them. When writing true personal experience stories stick to the facts as much as possible, but allow yourself creative license to craft the dialog and the story to entertain the reader. Just remain as true to the basis of the story as possible. For instance, don't add a dog to the story for drama and effect if there was no dog. And don't add in another person for additional dialog if the scene happened between only two people. Real life is compelling enough, and entertaining in a large enough way, to stick to the facts as much as you can while adding in enough elements to entertain the reader. What do I mean?

Let's say my husband was wheeling out one of our behemoth garbage cans to the curb for trash pickup day. Did he bring out the brown one first? The green? The blue? Does it matter? Not really, if it's not important to the story.

Or I write in a scene that I had on blue jeans, the ones tattered with a frayed hole in the left knee that I constantly stuck my finger into, pulling at the strings of white thread that tickled my tanned flesh underneath. The story takes place when I was thirteen, and I owned three pairs of blue jeans, all with various frayed edges and tattered bottom cuffs, several with holes in the back pockets, and even a pair so ratty my mother made me change every time she saw them. Do I remember which exact pair I had on that day when I ran away from home?

Some memories are so ingrained in our brain we recollect every tiny detail, others are not. Craft the story to entertain the reader with vivid, descriptive writing and don't worry if your memories don't match exactly to what a family member might recall. These are your memories, and your personal experience stories. Do the best you can.

I'll talk more about vivid, descriptive writing later on in Chapter 6: The Seven Steps to Stories that Sell.

Do you have a good understanding of a nonfiction short story? It's a true, personal experience, inspirational story usually between 1,000 and 1,500 words.

Ready to move on? Let's go.

CHAPTER 3

Do I Need a Formula?

Have you ever cooked without a recipe?

A little of this, a little of that.

A dash of this, a dash of that.

While following a recipe, adherence to the actual amount of the measured ingredients is often extremely important. Too much salt and the recipe will taste awful. Too much milk and it can be watery. Too much red pepper and it could light your tongue on fire.

It's a good thing my formula for writing short stories doesn't need to be quite that exact. But there are certain elements you will want to include to give your story the necessary ingredients of a solid, saleable, inspirational piece.

What are the ingredients? We'll get to that in a minute, but first, let's examine what a formula is. An informal use of the word "formula" in science refers to the general construct of a relationship between given quantities.

That makes sense for us because a short story must have a beginning, a middle, and an end.

But what makes a captivating beginning? What piques the reader's interest enough to want to continue reading?

What keeps the reader involved in the story, reading all the way through the middle? This is the point where many readers put down the magazine or book, bogged down in a story that drags or does not entertain. How do you develop the middle well enough to keep a reader engaged?

What leaves the reader with a satisfying feeling at the end? Have you crafted the story to a moment in time that the reader feels they have learned or experienced something through your words that might change them? Do they feel content when they close the magazine or book?

You need all of these elements in your nonfiction short stories. But how much of each?

For the purpose of writing inspirational, true stories, the P MS TO A T formula is not exact, but it is specific. You do not need the same amount of each of the above-named elements, but you do need them all.

Want to learn the formula?

We're almost there.

CHAPTER 4

What Came First, the Chicken or the Egg?

Before I get to the formula, I have a question for you.

Do you want to figure out where to find good stories to write?

Or do you want to learn how to write good stories that sell?

Ahhh…both you say! Good answer.

Let me ask another question: do you have a life?

Yes?

Then you have stories. If you think you don't have anything to write about, think again. Pick a topic, like one of the *Chicken Soup for the Soul* book ideas posted on their website. They want stories about … and there are many books always in development, I'll list a few here … Think Positive, Volunteering & Giving Back, Make Your Own Luck, and the Christmas Season. Do you have a dog or a cat? It seems every other year *Chicken Soup* does a book for dog and cat lovers. Think about it. Do you have a story you could submit to one of those books in development? I'll bet you do. And if those books are already closed by the time you read this, check the website for more topics.

Your memories are a treasure chest for stories. Close your eyes, lay your head back against a soft cotton pillow or the back of your tweed sofa, and think about your life.

What is it you can write about that will inspire others?

What has happened to you that is funny in hindsight but wasn't at the time?

What have you experienced that you'd like to share with others to give them hope or inspiration?

We'll go into mining the wealth of our memories when we talk about the Seven Steps to Stories that Sell.

Trust me. You have lots of stories to share.

And what about the second part of the chicken/egg question?

You want to learn how to write good stories that sell? That's what I'm going to share with you. It's quick and easy to remember.

The **P MS** TO A **T** formula will take you further down your writing career path than anything else I can teach you.

The market for short stories is always changing. What may be a viable avenue today could dry up tomorrow. And what isn't here today could spring up as a fantastic market tomorrow. Keep your eyes and ears open for possible places to sell your short stories, and then get busy, because this formula doesn't change. No matter what the years will bring, it remains tried and true.

Let's get down to it.

CHAPTER 5

The Winning Formula:
P MS to a T

Are you ready?

This is what you've been waiting for, and I won't disappoint you. I'm going to tell you the formula here, and then, when you read the Seven Steps to Stories that Sell, I'll show you how to put it into action in your stories.

I keep saying that, don't I? It's the chapter where I will teach you the most. It will be like attending one of my workshops at a writers' conference, only you'll already know the formula, and you'll have more than one story to study.

So you want to know what the P, the MS, and the T stand for? Here it is:

The Winning Formula for Writing
Nonfiction Short Stories that Sell

P   –   **is the story PROBLEM**

MS   –   **stands for MULTIPLE SCENES**

TO A T –   **to a TURNAROUND / TAKEAWAY**

It's easy. It's memorable. But how does it all work?

I'm going to go into detail with concrete examples. Just remember, you must have P MS TO A T whenever you sit down to write an inspirational short story if you want it to sell.

In fact, you can consider it the formula for a nonfiction full-length book as well. Try it with your own manuscript and see what I mean.

I've been writing for more than twenty years (I was a late starter), and I cut my teeth on writing true life stories. My first was a contribution to John Gray's *Mars and Venus in Love*, and shortly after I had a few stories accepted and published in my local newspaper that ran a True Life section. They even ran photos with the stories. What a thrill.

Years later, I wrote the book CHARLIE BEAR: *What a Headstrong Rescue Dog Taught Me about Life, Love, and Second Chances.* And guess what I used when writing the book? The same formula I shared with you. Why did it work in a nonfiction book? Because the whole book is one long STORY. It has a beginning, a middle, and an end.

Now let's learn how to apply the formula so you know how much of each ingredient to put into your story and how to craft it well.

I can't wait to share how it has worked for me.

CHAPTER 6

The Seven Steps to Stories that Sell and How the Formula Fits

What's being published out there? It goes without saying, but I'm saying it anyway. Study the market you wish to submit to.

It's important to read what comes out in print from the market you are targeting. For instance, *Chicken Soup for the Soul* does a variety of books delving into different topics. Watch the list and study the information paragraph underneath the title to get a feel for what they are looking for on each book topic.

The sister publications *Guideposts*, *Angels on Earth*, and *Mysterious Ways* are also great markets. Get the magazines, study what they publish, and decide if you have a story that could fit.

Many women's magazines also contain true life short stories.

I have had a lot of success writing for *Chicken Soup for the Soul* and also for *Guideposts* and *Angels on Earth*, which is why I mention these publications a great deal in this book. There is no other reason why I talk about them so much.

Each of the magazines mentioned above has a different target audience. Do you know who you are writing to?

Get a feel for what a market is looking for. Read the stories that are getting published. Is your story so very different you have never seen anything like it in the magazines or books you are targeting? That could be good, meaning it could capture their attention, or it could be bad, meaning it is a subject matter that doesn't go over well with their readers. It doesn't hurt to try, but be aware of your market and target readers. Practice and hone your craft to become a "fit" for that publication.

I like to put it this way:

If you were studying to be a CPA, and you have a love for numbers and crunching and making all the checks and balances work out to equal, you would take classes and workshops on how to become the best accountant you could be, right?

Or let's say you want to be a bartender. You'd need to know how to mix a great drink, how much of this and how much of that to shake or stir to just the right consistency. Wouldn't you always be tasting and testing? You would learn the skills of your trade.

Or maybe you want to be a belly dancer. You've seen the ladies shake and shimmy and you've even tried it yourself in your own living room. You run out and buy the waist chains, the hand clickers, the silky veil and balloon palazzo pants. And then you practice, practice, practice.

It's the same with writing short stories that sell. Your first one may fall flat. Your next may get an editor's second look but not be chosen for publication.

Will you give up? Or is this your passion?

If you are driven, determined, and believe in yourself, you will invest your time and effort in becoming a better writer. It is often the third or fourth or even fifth time of submission that gets you the prize of publication.

Consider my friend Lynne Leite. She attended my class "Writing Personal Experience Stories that Sell" in 2011, wrote a story for *Chicken Soup*, submitted it, but didn't get picked to be in that book. Did she give up? A resounding no. She submitted another story for another book, and that story was chosen and went to print. Lynne was a published *Chicken Soup* author.

But Lynne didn't stop there. Using the formula from my class, Lynne went on to sell 8 more stories to *Chicken Soup* over the next 18 months. Awesome? Yes.

Don't give up. Don't ever give up.

Now let's get into the steps.

Step 1: Find a Unique Story with a Distinctive Slant

Years ago, *Chicken Soup* had a call-out for a book for preteens. Here I was, in my (ahem….I won't say how old, but I wasn't a spring chick), thinking about what might interest a preteen boy or girl. Were the same things happening in their lives that happened in mine?

One thing I knew for sure: the editors would get lots of stories about the morning of the first day of school, the pimple that looked as big as a giant oak tree on the tip of their nose that rocked their world when they saw it in the mirror on school picture day, the first kiss behind the flagpole on the playground, the first Sadie Hawkins dance where everyone was a wallflower, the first time someone asked them out and daddy said no.

I wanted to write something different.

So I wrote about running away from home. That's pretty different, huh? In fact, so different, so edgy, I thought for sure they would never accept it. Especially the way I started the story.

From "Hot Potato/Cold Potato" in *Chicken Soup for the Preteen Soul* II

"I hate you!" I yelled, as I ran up the stairs to my room. Throwing open my dresser drawers, I pulled out a clean T-shirt and jeans, threw them in my backpack and ran back down the steps. Mom and Dad stood there, looking like they were in shock.

"Where are you going?" Mom asked.

"Anywhere but here," I shouted as I ran out the door. They weren't fast enough to grab me, and I slipped away into the night. It was cold, but my hot temper warmed me, and I didn't feel it. Not at first, anyway.

Was that going to fly with the editors? Was it too much? Did they want just pimples and teenage dreams? I decided to write the story and submit it. This cliché still holds true: Nothing ventured, nothing gained. The editors had

a committee of pre-teens read the stories to help in the selection process. Those kids voted on the ones they liked the best. My story was chosen to be in the book.

Want to know something else that happened with that story? It garnered the most emails ever from young girls who reached out to me. They said things like, "I wanted to run away from home, too, but then I thought of you," and "I decided my home wasn't so bad after all, and that I could make more of an effort with my mom and dad."

Those emails made me feel great.

There have been other times when I have searched my brain for a unique story, something unusual, something not everyone would think of writing about. For instance, for *Chicken Soup Celebrates Grandmothers* I wrote about traveling 2,000 miles with a rolling pin, containers of red, blue, green, yellow, and pink colored sugars and a container of red hots. Nestled in my suitcase in the bowels of the plane were Tupperware containers that held the pre-made sugar cookie dough and the sweet and delicious butter cream frosting. All were frozen and double wrapped in Ziploc bags.

When I landed and embraced my family, the fun began. Sons, grandsons, a brother, and nieces and nephews rolled out the dough in the shapes of Santas, reindeer, gingerbread houses, stars, and Christmas trees. Little hands pressed down firmly to get the reindeer's left hoof to come out right (we ended up with many a hoofless reindeer, but it didn't matter).

After baking, the assembly line began. The adults frosted and the children walked the line, spooning from each bowl holding a different color of sugar, a couple of bowls now also bearing sprinkles and those yummy red hots. Ooohs and aaahs and "Look at this one, Grandma" rang out across the tiny room, the many family members crammed around the kitchen table having a joyful time. Trays of cookies were proudly displayed at the end of the day with a dad vacuuming up the tile kitchen floor and an uncle washing the dishes in the sink.

Was it unique? Maybe not the decorating of the cookies (done in lots of families), but traveling 2,000 miles with frozen dough and frosting? That might have been a first for the editors. I don't know, but it is a true story, like all personal experience stories must be. I did every one of those things, and am still doing them today, more than 11 years later. It's a highlight of our family reunions.

That story titled "Make a Memory" was accepted into a small hardcover book titled, *Chicken Soup for the Soul Celebrates Grandmothers*. It held only 11 stories along with black and white photographs chosen by the editors and publisher. Later, when the publisher compiled a book of their 101 Best Stories of Christmas, "Make a Memory" was chosen for that book titled *Chicken Soup for the Soul Christmas Cheer*. Do you know how good I felt to be chosen the first time for the book of only 11 stories, but also to join the cherished picks for the 101 Best Stories of Christmas Cheer? It was a thrill of a Chicken Soup moment for me, I'll tell ya.

I challenge you to think deep. Beyond the ordinary and routine and mundane, to the frivolous, happy, spunky, quirky, touch-your-soul-and-heart moments. Share those.

How about the stories you tell around the table about the time when little Davey did this or that?

Or tiny Samantha woke up in the middle of the night and did something?

What stories do you reminisce about?

What events of your past or present make you laugh out loud?

Which stories are melancholy or chock full of memories?

What stories make you cry?

Those are your nuggets of story gold. Write about them.

Share the uniqueness that is you.

Step 2: Focus on a Single Event

The challenge we have as writers is to know what to put into the story and what to leave out.

For the story about running away from home, there were members of my writers group who insisted I explain in more detail why I wanted to run away. It wasn't enough for a couple of them to hear about moving from school to school, not fitting in. They wanted more. I thought what I wrote was enough.

Why? Because every preteen who considers running away is probably considering it for a different reason. Some might be the same as mine, but some might be different. To me, it didn't matter for the story and I didn't want to take up precious word count going into more detail. It was sufficient to explain in a general way why I felt the way I did, because the story was about running away and what happened when I left home, not the history behind it. Make sense?

Think about television shows and movies. If they don't engage you right away, you'll flip to a different channel. Do they give you tons of back story and reasons for why something is going to happen, or do they plunge you immediately into the riveting action, keeping you engaged and entertained?

You got it. They grab you and keep you engaged. So much so that you want to watch the show until the very end to find out what happens, right?

Your challenge is to stay focused on the single event you are writing about.

For that manuscript about running away, it was the park bench late at night where I curled up to sleep with homeless people all around, the halfway house where I had only a hard, dry, cold baked potato to eat for dinner, to the sun-filled day when my father found me and drove me home. All of the events I described in the story pertained to the main issue of running away.

When you write a story, feel free to just write it out, go for as long and for as many words as you need. Then go back and hone it down to the focus of the story itself. It's a challenge because you can become fond of every word you write and don't want to delete one of them. Be ruthless about looking at your story closely to see if it remains on topic, and ask other writer friends to look with you and offer suggestions. It would be fantastic if you were a member of a writers critique group. Someone else can see your story more clearly. Ever find that to be true?

Let's look at the making and baking of the Christmas cookies with the family. I didn't bring in all sorts of extraneous words that didn't stay on the story topic. In fact, that story was barely over 800 words but I believe it is rich in detail and vivid scenes.

Sometimes, when we think we need to add more, it is really less that will tighten and tone a story to what is necessary to captivate and engage the reader.

From "Make a Memory" in *Chicken Soup for the Soul Celebrates Grandmothers*

"Are you and the kids going to be home this weekend?" I asked my son. "I want to come up and see you guys."

"We'll be home. When can you get here?"

"I found an affordable flight on the Internet. I'll be there in three days."

"Cool. I'll tell the kids."

"I want to do something fun. Let's make Christmas cookies—the kind we used to make when you were a kid, the cutout ones that you bake and then decorate with icing and colored sugars."

"Yeah. I like those. And the boys will, too."

It would be a messy, fun, memory-filled weekend. Since every moment I spend with my grandchildren is precious, I didn't want to waste time going to the grocery store once I arrived at their house. Nor did I want to bend over a mixing bowl when I could be holding a child in my arms.

After that opening, the story continues with all sorts of detail surrounding the making of a memory. By the way, it's okay to "set up" the story by inserting a bit of back story for the reader. In the above example, that would be the paragraph that starts, "It would be a messy, fun, memory-filled weekend." Don't let this nugget of information for the reader go on too long, though, and don't make it the very first paragraph. More on that below in Steps 3 and 4.

We're going to analyze stories now in the coming Steps to help you see how the formula works. The objective is to help you to craft stories you can sell.

Step 3: Determine the Story PROBLEM

P – is the story PROBLEM

Ask yourself when you write your story: What is the story REALLY about?

We frequently think a story is about a particular event that happened, but if we look deeply we can find the true meaning of the story. That is the story PROBLEM, and the problem is the first element in the formula for a nonfiction personal experience short story that sells.

Why? Because if a story doesn't have a problem there is no reason for the reader to keep on reading. Let's say I started the story about running away with something like this:

Running away from home wasn't something I really wanted to do, but I did it anyway. Good thing I learned a lot because now I know home really is better. I'll never run away from home again.

Do you think a reader is engaged by that opening paragraph? In one short paragraph it TELLS everything: I wanted to run away, and I did. I learned from it, I came home, all is well, and I'll never do it again.

Does the reader need to read the actual story? Or even want to? There's no reason to. They'll move on to a story that piques their interest, one that is engaging, captivating, and riveting.

Your job as a writer is to engage your reader with a story problem preferably within the first two paragraphs. In the running away story, what's the PROBLEM?

In my workshop classes I ask writers to identify the problem when we read a story aloud. This is what has been described as the problem in the running away story:

She hates her parents.

She thinks life will be better somewhere else.

If you only looked at the first two paragraphs, you'd have to say the story problem is she hates her parents. Will the reader wonder why? Will they continue to read to discover why this young girl shouts "I hate you" and then runs out the door? Will the reader feel compassion for the parents, who are standing there slack-mouthed, unsure of what to do with a 14-year-old rebellious daughter? Are any of those questions raised in your own mind as you read the two opening paragraphs?

The story continues with the problem defined in a little more detail by giving you a little back story/insight into why this child is behaving this way. More on that later. But the problem must be right up front or the reader will not keep reading.

Make sense? Another way to define the story problem is to call it CONFLICT. A story must have conflict. Without it, there is no reason for a reader to remain engaged.

Let's look at the first couple of paragraphs in another story.

From "A Boy for Brutus" in *Meredith Books Along the Way*

"Are you going to take my dog?" the boy asked, his voice quivering. He stood behind his mother with tears in his eyes. I looked away as she scooped him into her arms.

"Remember what I told you, Tommy? We're moving to a small apartment, and we can't take the dog. This nice lady will take him."

"But why?" he wailed.

I tried to control my emotions. I felt bad for Tommy and his mom. The older kids would miss Brutus, she told me, but he was Tommy's dog, so it was toughest for him.

Do the first two paragraphs give you conflict? Do they present the story problem? That was a tough story to write. Brutus was an awesome dog. He loved his boy, and his boy loved him. You can read the remainder of the story at the back of this book and analyze it for our P MS TO A T formula.

How about two more examples of P – **is the story PROBLEM**.

From "Empowered" in *Chicken Soup for the Soul: Shaping the New You*

"You've got to be kidding," I hissed through clenched teeth as I tried on my favorite pair of pants. I lay on the bed, sucked in my stomach, pulled and tugged, but the zipper wouldn't close. In disgust, I tugged them off and threw them to the back of the closet. I fished out a long wrap-around skirt and tied it around my middle, then joined my husband downstairs.

"You look nice," my husband said.

"No, I don't," I shot back. "I'm fat." I caught a glimpse of myself in the hallway mirror. I didn't like the person I saw. How did I get this way? The weight started creeping on after the kids were born. But they were in their 30s now!

From "Bandit" in *Chicken Soup for the Soul: What I Learned from the Cat*

"Aren't you going to kiss me goodnight?" I said with a lump in my throat. My husband twisted underneath the sheet and gave me a peck on the cheek. Then he turned his back to me.

"Goodnight," he said without any emotion.

I lay there quietly, trying to escape the tension between us. We'd had a big fight, over nothing really, right after dinner. And now we were in bed without any resolution to it at all. I would have stayed up for hours discussing what was wrong. He didn't want to talk about it.

Can you pick out the story PROBLEM / the CONFLICT in those two examples?

In "Empowered" the woman is frustrated that she doesn't fit into her favorite pair of pants and angry at how she looks when she sees herself in the mirror. The Problem is her weight. The reader will wonder what she's going to do about it.

In "Bandit" the husband and wife have had a fight and have gone to bed without resolving it. The Problem is the wife wanted to talk about it but the husband didn't. The reader will wonder if they make up, and how, and if they get their marriage back on track.

Take note in the Bandit story I did not go into detail about what the fight was about, just a general comment that it was about "nothing really." And isn't every marriage filled with fights over "nothing"?

I love opening with dialog. I feel it brings the reader right into the story. But whenever I use dialog as my opening, it might be the third or even fourth actual paragraph that brings the problem into view for the reader. That's because dialog must be separately written paragraphs.

You must start a new paragraph when you change the person who is speaking. Take a look at the openings I've shown you and at the Study Stories at the end of the book. You'll see what I mean.

If you feel you have a good handle on **P – is the Story Problem**, let's move on to the next Step.

Step 4: Design an Opening Hook that Snags

This step delves a bit deeper into the **P – is the story Problem** part of our formula. You don't want to TELL what the problem is to the reader by stating it in two or three short sentences. Here's a bad example:

Everything that could go wrong did go wrong that Christmas. It was the worst Christmas of my life. It turned out okay, though, even after all I went through.

Instead, how about a bit of SHOW in the opening hook for the reader. Does this sound better?

"Mom, where are you?" Christie asked. I could barely hear her over the loudspeakers in the airport announcing yet another flight delay.

"In Denver, Sweetie," I said, holding my cell phone tightly to my ear.

"Will you make it home for Christmas?" she asked.

I could hear the break in her voice. At 12-years-old, she needed me. This was our first Christmas without her brother. Snow blew in sheets outside the floor-to-ceiling windows. I shivered in my thin sweater. "I'll be there, Christie, I promise." Inside my heart I wondered if I could keep that promise.

That's a quick example I made up for you. It's not from a printed story I have had published, but that doesn't matter. Take a paragraph you have written that sounds like telling, and change it around to SHOWING. Showing is all about helping the reader to feel as if they are right there … in the moment … in the reader's shoes.

Did you feel for Christie when she asked, "Mom, where are you?" And how about the Mom's response—do you feel her conflict, her problem?

This is what I mean about crafting an opening hook that snags the reader. Do you want to find out if Christie's desire came true? If her mother made it home despite the snowstorm raging in Denver? And what about the brother? Why are they without him this Christmas? I think I'll write the rest of the story to find out. Just kidding. lol

The best way to get a feel for opening hooks is to study them. Ask yourself as you read each example if you are engaged, if you want to read the rest of the story, if the opening hook piques your interest.

Opening hook from "A Port in the Storm" published in *Chicken Soup for the Soul: Teens Talk Middle School*

> "I hate this school. And I hate your stupid rules," I muttered.
>
> "We have rules for a reason, Miss," the principal said.
>
> He scribbled on some papers. I read it upside down—ONE WEEK SUSPENSION. That wasn't going to look so great on my record, but what did I care? This was my third school in three years—a middle school with the stupidest rules I'd ever heard of. Who knew leaving school grounds in the middle of the day would be such a big deal?

Opening hook from "Three Times the Love" published in *Chicken Soup for the Soul: The Gift of Christmas* sold at Walmart, and in *Chicken Soup for the Soul: Tales of Christmas* sold at Barnes & Noble, both in 2010

> "How come you got the purple one?" Judy asked as she looked at the red dress in her hands.
>
> "I don't know; ask Mom," Chris shot back.

Mine was pink. I always got pink. Everything Mom bought us was exactly the same, except for the color that is.

Opening hook from "Sweet Dreams" published in *Chicken Soup for the Tea Lover's Soul*

"Why does he always have big projects on a Friday afternoon?" I wailed when I walked in the door after work.

"What's the matter, Dear?" my mother-in-law said from the kitchen.

I threw my purse onto the counter. "Oh, my boss. He had me work late again. I didn't get out of the office until six o'clock. Now here it is almost seven. Why does he do that before the weekend?"

Opening hook from "Follow Me" published in *Chicken Soup for the Sister's Soul 2*

"Come on. Let's go," Chris whispered as she straddled one leg over the windowsill. The screen was on the floor, popped off with a screwdriver.

"I can't. We'll get in trouble," I hissed back.

"So what! It'll be fun," she said.

And just like that, I stuck my long, lean twelve-year-old legs through the open window and followed her into the night.

Opening hook from "Peter Pan" published in *Chicken Soup for the Soul: I Can't Believe My Dog Did That!*

"Rex, drop that!" He stood in the family room with a piece of paper between his two front paws. He had taken methodical bites out of it, then spit out the pieces first to the left and then to the right. A scattering of white lay in his wake.

I expected this from a puppy. But Rex was ten. Would he ever grow up and become a mellow, calm dog?

Opening hook from "The Perfect Solution" published in *Chicken Soup for the Soul: Family Caregivers*

"Honey, I miss you and all the children," Mom said, calling from her small apartment in Wisconsin to my home in California.

"I miss you, too, Mom. I'll see if I can get up there soon." She had lots of friends in her senior living complex, but she craved being with family, as all mothers do. And to be honest, I loved those warm hugs Mom so generously doled out. I wished there was a way to combine seeing Mom with seeing all the children and grandchildren at the same time, but Mom's apartment was so tiny that I had to blow up an air mattress to sleep on in the living room.

Opening hook from "Tick Tock" published in *Chicken Soup for the Soul: Divorce and Recovery*

There it stood on the front lawn. Tall, stately, mahogany wood and glass. Three brass weights hung from chains inside. A brass sun and moon rose and fell across shiny numerals.

My grandfather clock. My prize. My possession. Set out on the green grass like a discarded bath towel.

In my workshop classes we take one complete story and read it aloud. We only study one story, and not multiple opening hooks or problems or scenes, so you're getting WAY more than you would get by attending one of my workshops, plus you can refer back to these pages, and you don't have to take copious notes.

The reason we're going to read one complete story from beginning to end is because I believe it helps to see how the entire formula works together. I know we haven't discussed the remainder of the formula yet, but while reading the following story, look for these things:

The story PROBLEM, the MULTIPLE SCENES (we're going to discuss this in Step 5) and the TURNAROUND / TAKEAWAY (we'll discuss those in Steps 6 and 7).

Even if you don't quite know what you are looking for (except for the Problem, which we have discussed), let's read this story and then we'll go back and study it, looking for each of the formula's other ingredients.

Our Study Story:

Published in *Chicken Soup for the Preteen Soul 2*

1147 words

Hot Potato/Cold Potato

by B.J. Taylor

"I hate you!" I yelled, as I ran up the stairs to my room. Throwing open my dresser drawers, I pulled out a clean T-shirt and jeans, threw them in my backpack and ran back down the steps. Mom and Dad stood there, looking like they were in shock.

"Where are you going?" Mom asked.

"Anywhere but here," I shouted as I ran out the door. They weren't fast enough to grab me, and I slipped away into the night. It was cold, but my hot temper warmed me, and I didn't feel it. Not at first, anyway.

I hit the streets with my thumb out. Hitchhiking wasn't safe, but I didn't care. It was the only way I knew, at fourteen years old, to get away from them. We'd moved three times in the last four years, so I was always the new kid in class, the one who didn't know what chapter we were working on or what project was due next week. I was always playing catch-up and trying to fit in.

Worse than trying to fit in at school was trying to make new friends wherever we moved. There were cliques of popular students who knew each other since grade school. Then there were the geeks and jocks who just didn't seem to interest me. I wasn't athletic and didn't excel at anything, really. Just an average, high school kid looking for friends. Deep down inside I knew my parents loved me, just like God loved me, but it wasn't enough.

I slept curled up on a park bench the first night I took off. It was hard as a rock, and I was surprised to find that I wasn't alone. With my arms wrapped tightly around me for warmth, I huddled on the bench closest to the streetlight. Peeking through half-closed eyes, I could see other homeless people just like me, only they looked like they'd been there a long, long time. Some of them looked kind of scary, with dirty beards and baggy clothes. Some pushed grocery carts filled with their entire life's treasure. I didn't sleep much that night, and when the sun rose, I washed up in the park's restroom and hit the road.

By the end of the second day, I'd made my way to another city sixty-five miles away where I found a halfway house for runaways. I was tired, cold and hungry. By the time I got there, the kitchen was closed. All that was left on the table was a cold potato. I lifted it to my lips and bit into the wrinkled skin. It was crumbly and dry, and stuck in my throat when I tried to swallow. That night I slept on a cot in a room with four other runaways. It wasn't a whole lot better than the park. The cot was hard and the blanket was scratchy, and those other kids looked like they'd been there a long, long time. I tossed and turned all night.

The next day I changed into the only clean clothes I had and was shown how to use the washer and dryer to do my own laundry.

"The soap is over there," Carly told me. She was one of the other four runaways in my room. "Don't use too much, just half a scoop is all you need."

I wanted to ask her how long she'd been there, but she interrupted my thoughts.

"I've been here almost four months now," Carly said. "We have rules for what you can and can't do, so you better get used to it. You can't use the laundry before 8:00 in the morning and you can't watch TV after 10:00 at night. You have to be down at the kitchen table right at 12:00 and 5:00, or you don't eat, and you have to rotate chores every week. This is my week on kitchen duty. I help make lunches and dinners, and I clean up afterward. So don't go makin' a big mess in there."

"When are you going home?" I asked her.

"I don't know and I don't care. My parents know I'm here but won't come by to even talk to me, and so what! You got something to say about that?"

Carly glared at me as she talked.

"No," I responded, but I felt sad for Carly. Her parents didn't even care! I was scared. Maybe my parents didn't care, either.

Three days later, my dad showed up at the front door of the halfway house. I don't know how he found out I was there, but part of me was glad he did, though I wouldn't admit it out loud. After gathering my few things, we drove home in silence. I could almost see the questions running through his head. Why did she run away from home? What was so awful there that we couldn't talk about it? I could see by the look on his face that he felt responsible for all my anger and sadness. I regretted shouting at my parents the night I ran away. It wasn't their fault that I felt this way.

I had a long time to think as we drove those many miles home, and I wondered why I hadn't seen all the things Dad had done for the family. He was trying to make a better life for us, moving us from one city to the next so he could get a better job. He was doing his best to put clothes on my back and shoes on my feet. It was up to me to make the best of a new school and to open up to new classmates. Hanging my head in the halls and not talking to anyone who even said "hi" wouldn't help me make friends. Maybe I could make more of an effort to reach out to others.

When we finally reached our house, Mom opened the front door as we walked up the stairs. I smelled a roast cooking and knew there'd be hot baked potatoes to go with it. As I stepped inside, she opened her arms wide and I fell into them. Dad was right behind me and put his arms around both of us. Ordinarily, I'd pull away, but this time I didn't.

They both released me a few moments later, and that's when I saw the tears in Mom's eyes. I lowered my head and blinked twice really fast, trying to hide my own tears. I made a promise to myself not to hurt them like that again. They were doing the best they could. It was up to me to meet them halfway.

I knew the changes I had to make wouldn't take place overnight, but as I looked at my parents and felt the warmth in my house, I realized there's no place like home.

You were to look for the story Problem in the first two paragraphs (we'll give it three paragraphs to allow for the one sentence of dialog). The Problem is she hates her parents, and she thinks life will be better somewhere else. Is there conflict in this story? Her parents stood there, looking like they were in shock. What does that show you? That they weren't sure what to do with an unruly teenager who wasn't happy?

Does this story have a unique angle, a distinctive slant? Did you get involved in the story immediately through the opening hook? Did it snag you? Does the story stay focused on a single event? Now that you've had a chance to read the entire story, see if those questions can be answered affirmatively.

Now we're going to study how you go from an opening hook that has snagged the reader to keeping the reader engaged and riveted throughout the entire story. This is the danger area, the dreaded "middle" that often lags. It's where readers frequently stop reading because they are not entertained.

Let's help you with that in Step 5.

Step 5: Entertain the Reader with Vivid, Descriptive, MULTIPLE SCENES

MS – stands for MULTIPLE SCENES

The next important element to the formula is the need for vivid, captivating, descriptive scenes that move the story forward. Without that, a reader will find the middle bogs down with too much telling, not staying focused and on track, and not enough entertainment. Above all, a story must entertain the reader.

Keep in mind a television movie. If the opening hook doesn't keep you entertained you will flip the channel to find another station that does captivate you, or you might turn the television completely off. We do not want our readers to be turned off.

The key to keeping a reader entertained is through vivid, descriptive SHOWING scenes. A story must have scenes that describe what the story is about, "showing" the problem. You've had it drummed into you in writer's classes: SHOW don't tell. But how do you do that?

In our study story, the opening shows us what? Can you "see" the young girl? Do you feel for her? Can you relate to her? She crafts a "picture" for you—a scene.

Readers are transported through a scene as they read, through words you have written that take them there, to that point in time. They can visualize the story playing out like a movie on a big screen. Each scene takes the reader from one action to the next to carry the story along.

The opening hook could be called a scene, but for the sake of my stories I label that my opening hook, and move on from there.

Craft your story. Add spice. Make it sizzle. I try for 3 or 4 scenes in every 1,000 to 1,200 word story. Go back to the study story and look for the scenes. Where is it in the story you feel you can "see" the action? That's a scene.

What's the first scene you find in the story above? It's the park. Can you visualize the young girl curled up on a bench, arms wrapped tightly around her for warmth, as close to the streetlights as she can get? Can you visualize the homeless people milling about with grocery carts holding their entire life's treasure? That's Scene 1.

The next? It's a small scene, but do you see it in your mind? She's at the halfway house, she's tired and hungry and all that's left is a cold potato on the table. Can you see the wrinkled skin, how crumbly and dry it must have been and how it would have almost stuck in her throat? And her hard cot and scratchy blanket aren't much better than the bench in the park. That's Scene 2.

The next has dialog and it's the exchange in the laundry room with another runaway. Can you feel the other girl's righteous attitude over what the new girl can and cannot do while living there? How about her anger and even fear? Her parents know she's there but haven't even come to talk to her. Can you picture the two of them in that laundry room, the machines whirring and spinning, one giving the other quite a talking to. And what about our story narrator? Is she afraid? Maybe her parents won't come for her either. That's Scene 3.

And then there's home. Her mom opens her arms and our runaway falls into them. Then her dad embraces them both by putting his own arms around them. Our runaway doesn't pull away. Can you see the three of them together, the girl in the center and the parents trying to hold tight? And what about those tears? Can you feel them welling up in the young girl and particularly the mom? That's Scene 4.

A possible way to remember this is to say to yourself: Add in a "scene" so I can say I have "seen" the story happening before my eyes, I have "seen" the exchange between the young girl and the other runaway; I have "seen" the arrival home when her mother opens her arms wide. I see all this in my mind as I read the words the author has written. Each of those are a "scene" you have "seen" – make sense? It's a play on the spelling of the words, but if it helps you to remember, more power to you, right?

If you struggle with SHOW don't tell and crafting scenes for your story, practice taking a paragraph you have written and rewrite it with dialog, or give us a picture we can see in our mind as to what is taking place.

Here's an example of TELLING, not showing.

     The man hit the ball off the first tee about 285 yards. It was a short shot onto the green and he used a pitching wedge, getting it close to the hole. Sinking the putt, he recorded a 3 on his scorecard. Under par. A birdie.

Instead, let's try SHOWING that in a scene:

"Wow, John, you hit that drive a long way," Fred said to his playing partner.

"It's well past the 150-yard marker," John replied. "Could be the best drive I've had all week."

When they got up to the ball, Fred checked his rangefinder, which recorded 125 yards left to the green. "Nice drive. Right around 290 yards. Hit it close now and you'll have a chance to go under par on the first hole."

John chose a wedge, took aim, and swung. The ball arced nicely into the blue sky then fell fast onto the emerald, recently mown green. It stopped just short of the white flag waving in the gentle breeze atop the tall flagstick sticking out of the cup. "Nice," he muttered under his breath.

Fred stopped the cart on the concrete path, engaged the brake with a loud pop, and joined John on the green, both holding their putters. "Go ahead, sink yours, John."

John eyed it up, wrapped his large hands around the worn putter's grip, and took a smooth backstroke. The ball fell into the cup. "Sweet."

"Sweet indeed. A birdie on the first hole," Fred said, then two-putted for a par. "Nice way to start the game."

In that example, can you "see" the two of them on the golf course? Can you picture the swing, the little white ball in the air, the flag on the stick? And how about the relationship between the two friends? Are they buddies?

That's a quick example I made up for you. It's not from a printed story I have had published, but again that doesn't matter. Take a paragraph you have written that sounds like telling, and change it around to SHOWING. Showing is all about helping the reader to feel as if they are right there … in the moment … in that person's shoes.

A nice way to SHOW, don't tell, is to describe what is happening using the five senses: eyes, ears, nose, fingers, tongue. Bring in as much of them as you can.

The Five Senses:

TASTE – we describe taste by using our mouths and our tongues to show the flavor of a chili pepper, heat of a jalapeno, chill of ice cream, bitterness of a lemon, saltiness of peanuts, sweetness of iced cinnamon rolls, dryness of over-baked biscuits, crunchiness of potato chips.

SMELL – we describe smell by using our noses to show pungent aromas, sweet scents of certain flowers, acrid smoke or burning embers, scented candles, heavy perfumes, baking banana bread, roasting turkey, woodsy pine needles, salty ocean air.

HEARING – we describe hearing by using our ears to show pounding drums, whirring windmills, whipping winds, lapping water, tinkling chimes, raucous sporting events, the quiet hush on a golf course, laughter of a child, bellow of an angry old man, tinkling of bells, hush of a still night.

TOUCH – we describe touch by using our hands, feet, and skin to show the softness of a baby, the etched lines and wrinkles on an old woman's face, the silky brushed fur on a family pet, cold of a new snowfall, wetness of a falling rain, scratchiness of a wool blanket, softness of flannel pajamas, strength of a solid hammer, deftness of a paring knife, the prick of a thorn on a rose stem, the pinch of a too-tight girdle, the warmth of a loved one's hand in yours.

SIGHT – we describe sight by using our eyes to show the deep velvet darkness of the night, the bright eye-squinting light of the sun, glinting rays off the ocean, shadows behind the trees, dancing beams reflecting off of a mirror, dusk descending into twilight, shady areas offset by bright patches of sunshine, the light of a friend's smile, the happiness in a warm embrace between loved ones, courage in the set of a soldier's posture, defeat in a runner's loss at the finish line, elation when hoisting the winning trophy, a grandmother's love as she holds her grandbaby, a mother's love as she kisses her child goodbye.

The five senses in our Study Story:

Taste is when she bites into the cold, hard, wrinkled potato and it sticks in her throat.

Smell is when she sniffs the roast beef her mother is making.

Hearing is when the other runaway explains how to use the washer and dryer and admonishes her on what she can and cannot do while living there.

Touch is the hard bench the first night, the scratchy blanket at the halfway house, and the warm embrace when the girl and her parents reach out to each other.

Sight is when she peeks through half-closed eyes at the homeless people with dirty beards and baggy clothes pushing their life belongings in a cart, her dad's face as he drove her home.

I'm glad I had at least something that hit all five senses, but I could have done better on the taste sense and also on the smell sense.

Check your story after you have done your first draft. See where you can include something that touches on these senses in every piece you write. And don't expect perfection right away. Practice, practice, practice. That's the only way you'll get good at writing through SHOWING, not telling, to engage your reader.

MS – stands for MULTIPLE SCENES is an ongoing lesson you will continually work on. The more you write, and the more you think in scenes, the better you will become at the gift of being a good writer.

Let's move into Step 6.

Step 6: Develop the Story to a TURNAROUND Moment

Regarding this last part of the formula, I know it should say:

to a TT – to a TURNAROUND / TAKEAWAY

There are a couple of reasons I don't call it that. One, P MS TO A T is easier to remember than P MS to a TT. Two, it rolls off the tongue easily. Third, I like it better.

For the sake of this book, we have two of the Seven Steps to Stories That Sell devoted to the "to a T" part of the formula. I hope it doesn't confuse you. It makes perfect sense to me! lol

Let's get into it.

TO A T - to a TURNAROUND

You want the problem/drama/conflict to continue through the multiple scenes, moving the story forward using vivid, descriptive imagery all the way until almost the end of the story. At least two-thirds of the story comes BEFORE the turnaround moment.

The turnaround in a story is when the narrator learns something, or has an epiphany, or realizes she was thinking a certain way and it might be better to change. In other words, she "turns around." Her actions take a new tactic. Her words reflect her new attitude. Her feelings change.

In our Study Story, can you find the turnaround? Go back and look before you read on. See if you can determine where it happens.

Did you find it? The young girl's turnaround comes in this paragraph:

I had a long time to think as we drove those many miles home, and I wondered why I hadn't seen all the things Dad had done for the family. He was trying to make a better life for us, moving us from one city to the next so he could get a better job. He was doing his best to put clothes on my back and shoes on my feet. It was up to me to make the best of a new school and to open up to new classmates. Hanging my head in the halls and not talking to anyone who even said "hi" wouldn't help me make friends. Maybe I could make more of an effort to reach out to others.

Let's look at examples from a couple of stories to explain it further.

Here's a short one. It sometimes doesn't take much to "turn around" the narrator:

From "A Boy for Brutus" in *Along the Way: Real Life Moments Touched by God*

On the way, I felt excited. Brutus was with children again! Even though I would miss him, I knew he would be happy.

This next one is longer, but dialog usually does take more room. The best part of dialog is that it acts as a great scene:

From "Blue, Brown & Green for our Red, White & Blue" in *Chicken Soup for the Soul: My Resolution*

Time passed, and months later my husband stood in the kitchen after dinner. "What are you doing?" he said.

"Smashing this cardboard carton for Big Blue." I had it on the floor, with one foot holding it down while the other foot flattened the end.

"You, sorting trash?"

"Yes, and don't be so shocked. It doesn't take as much time as I thought."

"What happened to fussing about three separate containers?"

"I don't know. I guess I hated change. But now that I'm used to it, I love doing my part."

Do you feel the turnaround in both of those? In the first the woman admits she will miss the dog but she's excited he will be with children again. She turns around from being sad to being happy.

In the second the woman didn't like sorting the trash but now she's doing it. She turned around from hating it to doing her part for the environment.

When you write your stories, remember not to bring the turnaround in too quickly because once the narrator has that epiphany, or moment of change, the story is almost over. You want to keep the reader engaged to the end.

In our Study Story you'll discover three more paragraphs AFTER the turnaround. Sometimes there is only one. Let the story flow into what is necessary.

Do you need more on **to a T – to a TURNAROUND**?

Here's one more example:

From "Sweet Dreams" in *Chicken Soup for the Tea Lover's Soul*

> I felt myself relax as I sipped the tea, warmth flooding through not just my fingers and hands, but through my whole being. I felt calmer.
> "So this tea—it makes bosses go away?" I asked, smiling.
> She laughed. "No, nothing will do that. But it will make you forget about it for a little while."

In that example, the narrator was stressed over the boss at work. The tea turned her around to a feeling of relaxation, a calmness, to forgetting about work for a little while.

I think turnarounds will come easy to you in your writing. It's the natural progression of a story to the ending.

The final thing we want to craft in our stories is the last part of the formula: **to a T – to a TAKEAWAY**.

Step 7: Wrap Up with a Satisfying TAKEAWAY

TO A T - **to a TAKEAWAY**

When I talk about a takeaway, I'm talking about the feel-good endings on stories.

Do you ever read a story that has a downer ending? Inspirational stories cheer people up.

And don't you, as a reader, appreciate a solid, satisfying ending? I know I do.

You might say, "Yeah, but life doesn't always turn out that way. Life isn't always sweetness and bright light." And you'd be right.

Life doesn't always bring us the ending we would like, but our job as inspirational writers is to bring the reader to a resolution, a TAKEAWAY, that is upbeat. We want to end the story with something that gives the reader a warm feeling, a change of attitude for the narrator, or a way of looking at something differently, even if that means (as often happens in life) accepting things the way they are and making the best of them.

Go back to the Study Story. What do you think is the TAKEAWAY? Before you read further, go back and take a look. See if you can determine where it is.

Did you find it? The takeaway for the story comes in this paragraph:

    I knew the changes I had to make wouldn't take place overnight, but as I looked at my parents and felt the warmth in my house, I realized there's no place like home.

Do you feel a sense of closure to the story? Sure, the young girl has changes to make, and yes, it won't happen overnight, but do you feel good after reading the story?

Inspirational magazines and books are filled with real, true life stories that deal with hardships and troubling times. But the endings are always uplifting.

Take a look at a few more takeaways:

From "Tick Tock" in *Chicken Soup for the Soul: Divorce and Recovery*

We were two young kids married too soon, but we had many wonderful times together. Not one moment of our marriage was wasted. Each minute was the way it was meant to be. Each hour a blessing. We learned a lot about ourselves, about our loves, about our lives.

Life changes.

Tick tock.

From "A Boy for Brutus" in *Along the Way: Real Life Moments Touched by God*

I had only been a stepping-stone in this dog's journey through life. Now Brutus had a family again and, best of all, a boy of his very own.

From "Make a Memory" in *Chicken Soup for the Soul Celebrates Grandmothers*

The afternoon wore into the evening, and cookie after cookie disappeared from the trays. Little hands would reach up and choose just the colors they were looking for. It was a happy day. But the best part came as music to my ears when I heard, "Grandma, can we do this again next year?"

Your takeaway to your story must come at the end. Go for short instead of long. You also don't want to preach or hit them over the head with the "message" of the story.

For instance, in the Study Story I could have talked about how young people shouldn't run away from home, should always stay and work it out, that it is never a good thing to run away from something. The market for that book was pre-teens. Do you think they would want to read a story that preached at them? No one likes to be preached at. Instead, find a way to wrap up the story in a short paragraph with a feel good ending that doesn't tell people what to do.

Write it out. Read it aloud. Ask a friend who has read the entire story. Does the ending fit? Does it feel good? Is it just pasted on to make the story have a nice takeaway? It has to reflect the feelings expressed in the story, it has to make the reader think, "You know what? Maybe if this certain thing ever happens to me, maybe I can have a change of attitude, a change in the way I think about it, a change in the way I respond to the challenges of my life."

That's what you are going for. Helping others. Inspirational short stories about your life will entertain others, but they will inspire as well. And isn't that why you write? Okay, maybe you want to make a bit of money too—nothing wrong with that.

Ultimately, at the core of my being, the reason I write is to help others.

Look at the examples I have given you and then look at your own stories. See how you can update your writing to reflect the winning formula, like a friend of mine did.

Carin Leroy attended a conference in Florida where she came to both of my workshops. Although she had succeeded in being published in a few magazines, her goal was to be published by *Guideposts* and she wanted to enter the Writers Workshop contest that year.

"B.J.'s method was an easy reminder to check each of my stories to make sure I had all the elements editors like," Carin said. "After the conference, I pulled out some stories and began to rework them according to the P MS to a T formula. Then I submitted two different stories to the *Guideposts* contest and prayed my articles were good enough to be noticed by an editor. Several months later I received a message on my machine. An editor wanted one of the articles for the *Angels on Earth* magazine (a sister magazine to *Guideposts*). I had submitted that same story five years earlier and never heard a word back then. Now, they wanted to publish it. I'm sure learning B.J.'s formula was the main reason the story was noticed and accepted."

Take all you have learned in these Seven Steps to Stories that Sell and examine your own manuscripts.

I've placed a number of my published stories at the end of this book for you to study, looking for:

The Winning Formula for Writing
Nonfiction Short Stories that Sell

P   –   **is the story PROBLEM**

MS   –   **stands for MULTIPLE SCENES**

TO A T –   **to a TURNAROUND / TAKEAWAY**

Chapter 7

Rewrite Is My Middle Name

Now that you've learned the Seven Steps, and you've written the story, do you stop there? Not if you're a good writer. You take the first draft and revise it until it is better. The first stab at crafting a story sometimes leaves out necessary ingredients.

Do you belong to a writers group? Do you get feedback on your writing from other authors?

A lot can be said about having other writers read our work. They can spot things we don't see ourselves. Maybe our opening hook doesn't snag the reader enough, or possibly we have too much material in the "back story." Maybe we are doing too much telling instead of showing. How about our 3 or 4 scenes, do they keep the reader engaged? Do they entertain to that turnaround moment? Does the story elicit emotion in the reader? Does our takeaway resonate with the reader?

I've written a book on writers groups, devoting one section to face-to-face groups, a second section to online groups, and a third section on how to positively critique. The book is titled *The Complete Guide to Writers Group that Work*. Writers have told me it has helped them set up their own critique groups, as well as helping writers develop a working relationship that sees the members becoming published, professional authors.

Having the support, encouragement, and motivation of other writers can help to get us over the hump of feeling down when the responses we get are not positive. When we are part of a writers group, we also have other writers to share our elation with when we hear good news, like this note from a friend of mine, Judy DuCharme:

"God's plans are sometimes surprising. While snowbirding in Florida from Wisconsin, I decided to attend the Florida Christian Writers Conference and went to a presentation by B.J. Taylor. Using B.J.'s formula, and after quite a few rewrites, I submitted a story to the *Guideposts* Writers Workshop Contest. It's a story about my niece spending the night in the ocean and how God kept her safe. Out of 4,000 entries, *Guideposts* selected 12 winners. I was one of those winners and I was given an all-expense paid week in Rye, New York where I was trained to be a *Guideposts* writer. This has opened up so many doors and added so much to my writing. P MS TO A T is the basic pattern for inspirational storytelling. I really appreciate B.J.'s input and guidance. I doubt I would have won without it."

Many good writers, like Judy DuCharme, entered the contest. But what happens when a writer enters a contest and doesn't win? Here's what happened to me.

I attended a class on writing for *Guideposts* in 1997. In 1998 I sent in a story to the *Guideposts* Writers Workshop contest. I thought I had it down. I was confident. But I wasn't chosen.

There are many reasons an entry doesn't make "the cut." In the case of the *Guideposts* contest, they receive thousands of entries and they run the contest only every other year. I had to look at those odds. On top of that, there were bound to be many good stories out there. Many excellent writers. It's a daunting task to the editors to choose only 12 people.

When I didn't hear anything in 1998, I knew I didn't make it. They don't contact the thousands of people who submitted unless they are chosen. I was sad, but not entirely depressed. Heck, I was up against staggering odds. So you know what I did? I took the same story, yes, the same story, and reworked it. I revised it, looked at it with a critical eye to see what they were printing in the magazine, and how my story might fit, how I could make it better. Then I rewrote it, put a different title on it, addressed my cover letter to a different editor, and sent it out again in 2000. Again I didn't hear. In 2002 I did the same thing to the story. Didn't hear again.

I must admit all that reworking, revising, and reshaping turned me into a better writer. I had attended workshops on how to write personal experience short stories every year since 1998 and I cut my teeth on the art and craft of an inspirational short story by submitting numerous times to *Chicken Soup*. I was accepted multiple times so why wasn't I making it into the contest? I didn't give up. I kept on writing for those other markets and in 2004 I submitted that same story again to the *Guideposts* contest.

After trudging out to the mailbox one August day in 2004, I came back into my garage holding an oversized blue and white envelope that said *Guideposts* in the upper left-hand corner. I stood in front of my washer and dryer, ripped it open, and read the words, "We'd like to invite you to join us at the Writers Workshop in Rye, New York..." You should have seen me. "Oh, my gosh, oh, my gosh, oh, my gosh." That was all I could say. I was a babbling mess. It took eight years, but I was finally chosen and now I'm a *Guideposts* writers workshopper. Can you imagine the thrill?

As they say, the rest is history. I have written many stories for *Guideposts*, *Angels on Earth*, and other publications in addition to now having 40 stories published in the *Chicken Soup* line of books, an inspirational book titled *Charlie Bear: What a Headstrong Rescue Dog Taught Me about Life, Love, and Second Chances*, a compilation of heartwarming stories in *Sunny Side Up*, and my agent is working on selling my first fiction book (hint: it's about a young woman searching for love and the capricious and unruly puppy that helps her find it). And I'm not stopping there. I have many more stories within me.

What happens when a writer enters a contest and doesn't win? One of two things occurs.

The writer digs deep, looks at the possible reasons why and tries again, or the writer folds up into a shell—depressed, angry, confused—and never submits another piece of work.

Which writer are you?

Don't give up. Don't ever give up.

When sharing your story with others (preferably not your mom, sister, dad or aunt), try to get the unbiased opinions of at least three people. If those people are writers as well, all the better. When looking at the comments these three people provide you, remember The Rule of Three.

The Rule of Three

When one person offers an opinion on your story different from anyone else, say to yourself, "Hmmmm...that's one person's opinion." You don't need to change anything in your story based on the comment of one person, unless you like it and want to use it.

When two people offer the same opinion, you might say to yourself, "Okay, I'll look at that. They might have something there." You can decide to change it, or not.

When three or more people say the same thing about a point in your manuscript, you might want to handle it this way: "It's interesting three people felt the same way. I will take a definite look at that and probably make the suggested change. If it struck that many, it must be important."

By using this rule, you will find it releases you from the feeling you must change everything someone says about your work. It is your body of writing, your style, your inspirational story, so don't change something based on one person's opinion. But do take into account the way the story is told, the formula, and the opinions of three people. Do not change things on a whim, but consider every comment and suggestion.

In the beginning, as unpublished authors, we should elicit all the help we can get to make it sellable. I hope that's why you bought this book, and I hope you will reach out to others to help you to fine-tune your writing using the P MS TO A T formula.

THE RULE OF THREE

One person suggests a change—it is a single opinion.

Two people propose the same revision—look at it closely.

Three or more members react the same way—take a definite look at making the suggested change.

Chapter 8

Titles Are Important

Titling a manuscript is an art. And creative art is a work in progress.

A title is usually the last thing I put on the story. Why? Because when reading the story again, out loud, I find the title right there in the manuscript in the words I have written.

Single word titles I have used include:

Bandit

Tina

Empowered

Toots

What do you think of those and the ones in the list below?
I have many more, but this is a good representation of titles
I have used on published stories:

> *Popcorn and Dirty Bare Feet*
> *Shaken and Stirred*
> *A Boy for Brutus*
> *Chocolate Covered Love*
> *Ebb and Flow*
> *Candy Apple Sweet*
> *More Than a Game*
> *Hot Potato/Cold Potato*
> *The Missing Ring*
> *ttyl*
> *Peace for Pickles*
> *More Than Coincidence*
> *Sweet Dreams*
> *Three Times the Love*
> *A Leap of Faith*
> *A Kick in the Keister*

And my longest title yet:
Blue, Brown & Green for Our Red, White & Blue

Titles come to me when I start the story, but I change
them after finishing the story, reading the story again, and
determining what the real gist of the story is. Then I put
the title on it. I don't want to give it away totally for the
reader in the title of the piece, but I do want to entice them
to read.

Which of the above titles pulled you in? Which didn't appeal to you at all? Which would you like to read if you had the opportunity?

If you prefer short titles, then go for a word or two. Look at the Table of Contents in most magazines and compilation books. They have limited space so consider the length of your title when submitting your story. Shorter is always better. I did extend myself with the Blue, Brown & Green for Our Red, White & Blue and I thought the editor might want to change it, but she didn't.

On the subject of titles, be prepared for a title change. I have had a few titles changed after a story has been accepted and I readily agree to the revision. Why? Because I want the story published. I'm not married to the title and the editors know what they need. For instance, I submitted a story to a dog book with the title, "Would He Ever Grow Up?" and the editor asked if she could change it to "Peter Pan" because another writer had sent in a story with a similar title to, "Would He Ever Grow Up?" Of course, I said yes to the change. Not a big deal.

Print out your finished story, read through it slowly, and highlight in yellow a nugget, a phrase, a meaning that catches your eye as a possible title. Then choose what best suits the work and teases the reader a bit to capture them and draw them in. This is another one of those times when practice, practice, practice comes into play. Ask others to help if you aren't good at titling your work.

Look at the titles on the story samples I have included at
the end of this book. Did the title capture your attention?
After you finished reading, did you feel the title fit the
piece? Could it have been better?

Chapter 9

How Do I Make My Story Stand Out?

Standing out to editors involves all of the Seven Steps:

- Submit a **unique** story with a distinctive slant.
- Focus that story on a **single** event.
- Put your story **problem** right up front.
- **Hook** the editor from the start.
- Keep the editor entertained through **multiple scenes**.
- Develop the story to a **turnaround** moment.
- Help the editor feel that satisfying **takeaway** ending.

There are a few things you also need to do.

First, format the story professionally. Years ago everything was submitted by U.S. Mail. It was extremely important to have your work look professional, with a cover letter and the manuscript formatted correctly. Even though you frequently submit via email today, I recommend doing everything you would have done years ago. Be professional in your cover letter (now your email cover), and use correct formatting in the manuscript you attach to the email. This will convey to the editors you value their time and want to make their job easier. The more you endear yourself to editors, the more they will want to work with you.

When sending your manuscript via email as an attachment, be sure your entire contact information is in the upper left-hand corner. That would look like this:

Jane Smith
100 Writer Street
Publication, ME 29806
Phone number
Email address
Website address if you have one

Single space the information then drop down a couple of lines and put the word count on the left-hand side. Then drop down a few more lines and center the title on the page. Drop down two more lines and put your byline, like this:

1149 words

TITLE OF STORY

by Jane Smith

Then start the story.

Number the pages and use either a footer, a header, or both. The header could state your name, then a slash with the story title.

Jane Smith/Title of Story

Set this up using the "Header" feature in Word and have it begin on page two of your manuscript. There is no need to have it appear on page one as the information is already there. Use the "Footer" feature in Word and center the page number at the bottom of each page. You can start the numbers on page one, or begin on page two.

I personally like to do a header because it includes my name and the title of the story. In case the pages are printed out and they become jostled and mixed up, the editor or reader can put them back in order easily.

Second, look like a pro. Format your story with one-inch margins all the way around and double space. This helps an editor, who reads stories for a living, have more ease in reading yours.

Let's talk about online submissions where you're inserting a Word document into a form. Say they ask you to cut and paste your story into a small box. Be sure you follow the directions exactly, filling in all information they ask for above or below the box.

When you submit your story into a small box in an online form, go to your Word document and "Select All." This will copy all of your manuscript, including the contact information in the upper left-hand corner. The header or footer will probably not follow through to the small box, but that's all right, and oftentimes the formatting of double spacing, indenting, etc. will also be lost. Cut and paste your entire document into the box and check it afterward for how it looks. I like to be sure there is a separation between paragraphs, but you could also leave it alone, since the editors will work with the story after it reaches them.

Third, write an informative bio.

Have you read the bios at the back of many books? I like to read a story and then go immediately to the back of the book to read the writer's bio. It gives me a bit more information on the author and makes me feel closer to him or her.

Bios are almost always listed alphabetically, so begin the bio with your name. Most of the time, a bio will state contact information so a reader can write to that author or look up his or her work. I really love that feature and it is included in many compilation books.

A bio can feel daunting to write. Talk myself up, you say? Give myself a pat on the back? Consider the bio an easy way for someone to get to know you a little bit and get in touch with you. Don't let it seem too complicated. It's not.

Write your bio in the third person. That means you write it as if you are talking about someone else. For instance, you are writing your own bio but you would not say "I volunteer at the local ..." You would say "Jane Smith volunteers at the local ..." Continuing on with "She lives in Writersville, ME with her husband and two cats. You can reach Jane at xxxx. com."

I'll give you examples of bios of my own in a moment, but first I'd like to suggest you write your bio boilerplate and then change the first line each time you submit to a different book. Here's why.

I like my bio to relate to the book the person is reading. If it is a dog book, my first line will state something related to the story about a dog I wrote for the book. If it's a book on being a grandparent, my first line will state something related to the story about being a grandparent. After the first line, the bio becomes boilerplate for me. I update it periodically if things change. I have fine-tuned this standard bio to give my contact information in as few words as possible. And that's not easy to do.

Work on yours and see what I mean. Most bios must be kept to 50 words or less. A challenge, but you can do it.

Take note that my first lines are different, but the rest is the same.

BIO examples.

From *Chicken Soup for the Soul: Grandmothers* (44 words)

B.J. Taylor loves talking to her grandsons via the Internet. She's an award-winning author whose work has appeared in *Guideposts*, many *Chicken Soup* books, and numerous magazines/newspapers. You can reach B.J. through her website at www.bjtaylor.com and check out her dog blog at www.bjtaylorblog.wordpress.com.

From *Chicken Soup for the Soul: Shaping the New You* (49 words)

B.J. Taylor loves how she feels and looks, which motivates her to make wise choices. She's an award-winning author whose work has appeared in *Guideposts*, many *Chicken Soup* books, and numerous magazines/newspapers. You can reach B.J. through her website at www.bjtaylor.com and check out her dog blog at www.bjtaylorblog.wordpress.com.

From *Chicken Soup for the Soul: I Can't Believe My Dog Did That!* (43 words)

B.J. Taylor finds Rex adorable, even when he's capricious. She's an award-winning author whose work has appeared in *Guideposts*, many *Chicken Soup* books, and numerous magazines/newspapers. You can reach B.J. through her website at www.bjtaylor.com and check out her dog blog at www.bjtaylorblog.wordpress.com.

From *Chicken Soup for the Soul: I Can't Believe My Cat Did That!* (45 words)

B.J. Taylor can't believe how Red helped her find romance again. She's an award-winning author whose work has appeared in *Guideposts*, many *Chicken Soup* books, and numerous magazines/newspapers. You can reach B.J. through her website at www.bjtaylor.com and check out her dog blog at www.bjtaylorblog.wordpress.com.

From *Chicken Soup for the Soul: Family Caregivers* (47 words)

B.J. Taylor continues the family tradition at the hotel suites to this day. She's an award-winning author whose work has appeared in *Guideposts,* many *Chicken Soup* books, and numerous magazines/newspapers. You can reach B.J. through her website at www.bjtaylor.com and check out her dog blog at www.bjtaylorblog.wordpress.com.

My bio is included at the bottom every time I write a story. Doing it right away gives me the pleasure of knowing it is done when the story is accepted for publication. Notice I didn't say "if" the story is accepted. I try to think positive and believe in myself and my writing. I craft the first line of my bio to slant toward the story I have written, paste in the boilerplate information, and check to be sure it is 50 words or less.

I let the bio go with the story when I "Select All" and insert it into the little box for submissions. At times, when the story is accepted for publication, the authorization form requires a signature with the bio included again. That's all right. No problem. I open my word document, copy and paste, and voila! It is done.

What if an editor wants to make changes to your story?

You might wonder about revisions after you have submitted a story. That is a definite possibility, and more than likely a probability. Editors will tweak your stories, change words, cut a line or two, or use more active voice instead of passive. When your story is chosen for publication you will most likely receive the story already typeset as though ready to go to the printer. The editor will ask for your approval. It cannot go to print without it.

Be sure to respond promptly to an email from an editor. At first you may be asked a question or two on your story, then you might be told your story is in the running to be chosen for the book, then you will receive the story to approve. Be sure you reply to each email as quickly as you can by doing exactly what they ask for. Does the editor want a quick response as in "received" or do you need to complete an authorization form and send it in? Do you need to read the attached story and approve it? Do whatever is asked of you in a professional manner.

If your story has been shaped a bit by an editor or someone on staff, look at it as a guide to improving your writing. If there is something glaringly wrong in the story, a revision an editor made that must be addressed, discuss it with the editor via email.

In all the stories I have had accepted with *Chicken Soup for the Soul*, only one time have I had to point out an error in a story going to print. It was a hockey piece and the error had something to do with the year of an important game.

The year was corrected without a problem. If it is a small adjustment which does not affect the story adversely, I don't even mention it. I allow the editors to do their job. If I have the honor of being accepted into the book or compilation or magazine, I do what is required to make that happen.

Stand out by being professional, flexible, and open to revisions and suggestions.

CHAPTER **10**

How Much Money Can I Make?

I learned something valuable years ago.

Give 'em what they want.

I learned this little lesson (maybe not such a little lesson) a long, long time ago. John Gray had released *Men are from Mars, Women are from Venus* and was looking for ordinary people to tell him how his book had made a difference in their lives as a couple. Unpublished, full of hope, but not optimistic, I sent in five pages of manuscript, single-spaced. (I know, single-spaced, the biggest no-no. Now I would have formatted correctly, but that was eons ago.)

When a letter arrived from his editing staff requesting permission to publish my work, I was on cloud eleven. I couldn't believe it. How did my writing make it? In my head, I knew the answer. Using the terminology from the first book John Gray wrote I made references to his techniques.

I gave him what he wanted.

My happiness soared even higher when the galley of my work arrived by Federal Express. This was the stuff I'd read about that happened to other writers. Not to me.

Mars and Venus in Love was soon released. I still can't believe I'm in that book. Me. Little 'ole me. He didn't pay me a dime. He didn't give me a byline. But hey, I know I'm in there, and that's what matters.

Sometimes it was hard to keep going in those early years of writing, but I knew if John Gray liked my writing, then maybe I *could* make it out there. I didn't get paid in cold hard cash for that contribution, but I got something even more valuable. A boost to my ego. A lift to my self-esteem. Those things were worth more to me than a fistful of green dollars I would have blown in a fast food restaurant or the nearest grocery store.

You could say that first sale was priceless. It's where I learned to Give 'Em What They Want.

Writing stories has been my life's work as a writer. Isn't everything we do a story? We tell stories when we talk to others, we share stories around the dinner table, we even develop the stories in our minds and many of us craft dreams into novels.

For me, I write mostly about true life events, but in story fashion with a beginning, middle, and end. When I first started years ago I didn't make money on my writing, but that was okay because I knew I was learning. I was paying my dues. Editors were working with me, I was developing my writing style, I was teachable and eager to apply the lessons I learned. And the hardest lesson was when I was not accepted. I would study the story and try to discern why it was not chosen for publication. I submitted over and over again, and did not give up.

Along with submitting to markets that did not pay at all and receiving gratification when I was finally accepted, I began to branch out to markets that paid a small honorarium. Like the True Life section in my local newspaper, the *Orange County Register*. The editor loved the stories I sent in, but the newspaper had a tiny budget. I received $50 per printed story. Fifty bucks was a big deal. It still would be to me today. I recently sold two short stories, both around 1,000 words, to a compilation book for $250 each. And I have received $100 to $150 for stories of around 250 words from other publications. It all depends on the publication's budget.

Do I wish I was paid more? Of course I do. And I have markets that do pay me more, but it took me a long time, and a lot of hard work, to get my writing to the level of acceptance in publications that pay a higher fee.

In the beginning, work on getting your stories out there for the exposure and the experience. Look for paying markets and don't be afraid to submit to ones that seem out of your reach because you just might make the acceptance bracket. But until you do, keep learning.

One of the biggest markets for fresh, real life, personal experience stories is the *Chicken Soup for the Soul* books. They tend to average 10-12 books per year that go to print. There are 101 stories in each and every book. How many chances does that give you to get a story into the book? One hundred and one. Great odds, wouldn't you say?

I don't make it into each book I submit to, but I do try. Each time there is a callout for a book I search my brain and my file of stories. A recent callout was for "Dreams and Premonitions." I wondered if I had an inspirational story to submit. I thought I might. It involves a dream I had about my dad after he passed away and how he led me from room to room crammed with paraphernalia stacked from floor to ceiling. These were all the "things" in our lives, the items we consider must-haves. At the check-out line when Dad and I left, I had two or three things in my hands. He had shown me what was really important, and it wasn't all those things I thought I needed to be happy. I don't know if it will make it into the book, but I will write it up to the best of my ability and send it in.

Let's say you make it into a *Chicken Soup* book. Do you know what they pay? Currently, you will receive a check for $200 when the book comes out in print, PLUS you will receive ten free copies of the book. That's pretty nice. You can give them to family or friends as gifts, or sell them to make additional money.

What do other markets pay? It varies considerably. A story accepted into *Guideposts* or *Angels on Earth* could garner you a few hundred dollars or more, depending on the length of the story. Those of you who have aspirations of becoming a *Guideposts* writer, and you are submitting to the Writers Workshop Contest held every even-numbered year, can hope for a larger paycheck down the line. Once you are a winner of that coveted contest, you become a *Guideposts* writer, sometimes doing stories on assignment, or submitting your own for publication. The compensation moves up the ladder for you at that point, and you can make a nice sum of money per story (better than the $50 I made when I first started out).

There are many women's magazines out there but you will need to do your homework to find out if they accept true life, personal experience stories. Get your hands on a couple of issues of a magazine you want to write for, study the stories, then write one and send it in. Check out *Family Circle, First, Glamour, Good Housekeeping, More, Oprah, Parents, Redbook, Self, True Confessions, True Story, Woman's Day,* and *Woman's World*. Big name glossy magazines will pay many hundreds or even thousands of dollars for an accepted piece.

I have tried several of those markets, and have been published in *Victorian Homes* and *Romantic Homes*. The pay was good for the work I submitted. I've been published in *Writer's Digest*, the now defunct *Southern California Home & Outdoor* magazine, wrote a column for *On the Mountain* magazine, contributed to the *Guideposts Miracles* series, *Meredith Books Along the Way* series, and in *Lexus* magazine (with a one-page editorial and a photo of my dog Rex). The key for me has always been diversification.

Invest your time to learn all you can about submitting to different markets, give the editors what they are looking for by studying the magazine, and then professionally submit a story for consideration. Again, nothing ventured, nothing gained.

Chapter **11**

Ghostwriting? What's That?

A ghostwriter helps someone who is not a writer bring his or her story to light.

Many people don't know that stories about professional athletes, actors, actresses, television personalities, and various other well-known people are not written by those people. A reader who picks up a magazine with a top name celebrity's photo on the cover might think the celebrity wrote the story inside. In effect, it is the celebrity's words, but someone else pulled those words together and the editors brought the story to print.

Ghostwriting means a writer interviews the celebrity, formulates the story, submits it to the editors of the magazine or publication house if it is a book, and the story is then revised, closely edited, and eventually goes to print. The celebrity approves the story before it goes to publication, that celebrity's name is above the story as the byline, and photographs regularly accompany the story as well (approved by him or her or the celebrity's public relations department). The writer's name does not appear anywhere as the author of the story. For the sake of this book and this formula, we will stick to nonfiction short stories and not discuss ghostwritten books.

Let's say you know someone who has a great story to tell, but the person is not a writer. They wouldn't know the first thing about a story problem, or multiple scenes, or how to bring a reader to a turnaround and then a takeaway. But you do, and you decide to interview the person and submit the story. You are aware of your role as a ghost in the process.

Years ago it was common for many magazines to accept "as told to" stories. You would submit the story with that person's name as the author, then underneath his or her name you would write "as told to" with your name. The reader then understands the story is about that person but it was written by another person. The trend in many markets has been to move away from "as told to." True, real life stories for many publications must now be written by the person submitting. But if you want to help someone write a story, help that person to submit the story, put his or her name on the top as the byline, many places will accept that. Just know you, as the ghostwriter, do not receive byline or name credit at all when the story goes to print. The writer, you, would be paid a fee for helping to bring the story to print and that is often enough for a ghostwriter. It is about the helping aspect and not about the byline or the money.

Make sense? What we have to remember is this: when we help someone write a story, the formula is the same. It is still P MS TO A T.

When I craft a story for someone else, I interview to get the information needed to develop a great opening hook, compelling scenes, a turnaround that resonates with the author and the reader, and a takeaway based on what the author learned. After an interview I have copious notes that I transcribe, going back again and again to my highlighted pages and finding those scenes that make the story come alive using the five senses.

The biggest part for me of ghostwriting is *becoming* that person I am writing for. I take a photograph and prop it up near my computer, and then pretend I am that person. I try to feel what that person felt when the events occurred. I write from that person's point of view because all ghostwritten nonfiction stories are told in first person, like if I were writing it about myself.

I interviewed a gentleman who had been on a boat when the tsunami hit Thailand in 2004. When I sat down at my keyboard after the interview I pretended I was him. I closed my eyes and "saw" the boat he was on, the wave approaching and his feeling of helplessness, the longtail boats, the thin strips of sandy beach now gone, all the inhabitants who had been enjoying the day also gone. Empathy, compassion, emotion, and sensitivity bring me close to my subject and to the ability to write the story.

The challenge when ghostwriting is the same as when writing our own stories and that is to determine what goes into the story and what stays out. An interview can produce so much material it is difficult to determine what scenes to use out of so many. Our objective is to feel the emotions of the story and choose wisely. Ultimately, it will be the editors of the publication who decide if the story goes to print. They also work with the celebrity to revise the story to the point of approval. Our job as a ghostwriter is to give the editors the best story we can.

Does a ghostwriter get paid? Most of the time, yes. A publication frequently pays from their normal pay scale for a story brought in. That could mean a couple of hundred dollars to possibly much more.

The author of the story frequently receives an honorarium. I'm not sure what a celebrity would receive because I have never done a really big name author's story, but I would imagine it is more about the exposure in the magazine than the money.

Does all that make sense? A ghostwriter helps someone who is not a writer bring his or her story to light. Do you want to be a ghostwriter? Keep in mind you still need to craft a compelling story. Always use P MS TO A T.

Chapter 12

Would You Write to Me?

Did this book help you? I'm eager to hear your thoughts. Email me at bj@bjtaylor.com.

Do you have an exciting publication success you'd like to share? I'd love to hear from you.

I started out like most of you, submitting to non-paying markets. Those acceptances gave me the encouragement I needed to search for paying markets and the moxie to submit to them. And boy, was that a happy day the first time an actual check came in the mail addressed to B.J. Taylor. I felt like a real writer. I made it.

And now I'm making it in many other ways, but I have not forgotten where I came from. Inspirational, personal experience stories are the backbone of my writing career. Even with books published, speaking at writers conferences across the U.S., teaching workshops and helping others, I still submit short stories to numerous publications.

After all, isn't STORY what our world is all about?

A quick test for you: Can you remember, without looking back, what the P stands for? The MS? The T?

Good job if you did. This is what you need to remember each and every time you write an inspirational, nonfiction short story. Post the formula where you see it every time you write a personal experience story until it becomes automatic.

A few words from Sharron Cosby:

"When I returned home from a conference after learning B.J.'s formula, I put it into practice. The formula worked as I wrote about the Problem in Multiple Scenes, and provided a Turnaround and Takeaway for the reader. Using the formula, I crafted a story and sent it in to the *Guideposts* Writers Workshop Contest. My story didn't land me a spot at the winner's table, but it did usher me into the January 2015 issue of *Angels on Earth*. Following the formula works. Try it and experience the success of manuscript acceptance."

I was thrilled to hear from Sharron about her acceptance. I LOVE to hear from writers. Tell me how it is working for you. Share where you are published. I will grin with you each time you sell a piece of your work.

It is my hope if you do find yourself at a writers' conference where I am teaching that you stop me and say "hi."

And if you like this book, you could write a review on Amazon or spread the word to other writers. Reviews are greatly appreciated and so is word-of-mouth advertising.

Last, if you want a dose of inspiration, sign up for my Taylor's Tips Newsletter, a once-a-month unobtrusive newsletter sent via email. Go to www.bjtaylor.com and look on the right-hand side for the little box, then insert your email address. Or send me an email and I'll be happy to add you to the list. Just say: "Sign me up."

Thank you and may you have a bounty of blessings in your life.

STUDY GUIDE STORIES

I've placed six of my published stories here for you to study. See if you can identify the opening hook, the story problem, how many scenes there are, where the turnaround occurs, and the satisfying takeaway.

I haven't given away the P MS TO A T—unless we have studied part of the story in chapters above—but if you'd like to know the detailed answers, they are included at the end of the book.

Learn all you can. Add the winning formula to your writer's toolbox. Then go forth and write great stories that sell.

Published in *Chicken Soup for the Soul: My Resolution*

917 words

Blue, Brown & Green for Our Red, White & Blue

by B.J. Taylor

"You've got to be kidding," I raged. "I'm not going to separate our trash into three different containers. Forget it."

"It says here we'll be fined if we don't," my husband countered.

"Well, I'm not going to," I stubbornly replied. Chicken bones, potato peelings, cardboard cartons, plastic milk jugs; I put all of it together in one bag into one trashcan every night. That's the way I'd always done it, and that's the way I wanted to keep doing it. None of this fancy-schmancy sorting for me.

The flyer that came in the mail from our disposal company was colorful and enticing...a new recycling effort in our city; better for our landfills; less waste. Yeah, but what about my time? They wanted yard clippings in the green cart, recyclables in the blue one, and other trash in the brown one. All of this would take so much extra work. I tossed the brochure on top of the empty soup cans in the garbage.

The bins arrived on a Thursday a few weeks later. You could hear the new energy-efficient behemoth trucks lumbering down the street.

With a whoosh and a screech, the truck stopped in front of each house and, using a mechanized lift, deposited a blue bin at the curb. Then the lift rode up the track to the top of the truck, grabbed a green bin, brought that one down, and repeated the process for a brown one. Three huge, 95-gallon plastic bins on rolling wheels now sat in front of every home on the block.

"I'm not happy about this," I complained to a neighbor as we started wheeling them one-by-one into our backyards. They had a large handle on the back and a smaller one in front for maneuverability, but to me they were anything but maneuverable. They were monsters.

"Me, neither," she said. "They're too big."

"Yeah, and wait until they're full. They'll not only be big, but heavy."

I wheeled the first one through our side gate and surveyed the spot where we used to keep two regular sized trashcans. These monstrosities wouldn't fit in the old location. I moved a wire shelving unit where we kept gardening supplies, lugged the dog house from the dog's favorite corner and squeezed it in tight by the shed that held shovels and rakes. After more juggling, I managed to cram Big Blue, Big Green, and Big Brown next to the hoses and extra potting materials.

I stepped back and looked at them. "I hate these things," I mumbled to myself. They changed the way our backyard looked, like a ketchup stain on a white shirt.

That weekend we did some yard work. Weeds, dead pruned roses, some tree limbs cut down.

"Where does this stuff go?" my husband asked. "Is this supposed to go in the green one?"

"I guess so. It says 'yard waste' on it," I replied.

"What about the dog droppings? Is that yard waste, too, or something else?"

"I don't know," I said with half a smile. "Should we put it in the brown one since it's the same color?"

"You got me."

We finally decided to keep the green one strictly for prunings and grass clippings. "Okay," I said, "that was an easy decision. Now what about this big blue giant? What goes in there?"

"The small print on the top says: cardboard, plastic, paper, glass bottles and cans."

"Well, we can put cardboard boxes in there from packages delivered to the house."

"Right," my husband said. "And how about newspapers after you read them?"

"Those I put out by the mailbox on trash day for the guys that drive around. I'd hate to stop helping them. I think they make a few bucks by turning them in or something."

"Okay, well laundry detergent or plastic milk jugs, with the caps or lids off. And they say to wash out and flatten aluminum cans."

"No way. I have a hard enough time getting dinner ready without washing out a metal can before I throw it away."

"I'm just reading what it says. Don't jump all over me."

"I'm not, but this is ridiculous."

On trash collection day I wheeled out Big Brown and Big Blue. There wasn't much in Big

Green so I left that one behind until it had more in it. Big Brown was heavy and muscling it down the driveway and out to the curb made my muscles strain.

Time passed, and months later my husband stood in the kitchen after dinner. "What are you doing?" he said.

"Smashing this cardboard carton for Big Blue." I had it on the floor, with one foot holding it down while the other foot flattened the end.

"You, sorting trash?"

"Yes, and don't be so shocked. It doesn't take as much time as I thought."

"What happened to fussing about three separate containers?"

"I don't know. I guess I hated change. But now that I'm used to it, I love doing my part."

"That's my girl," my husband said, when he took me in his arms and hugged me. "And look at those muscles you're getting. Almost as big as mine."

"Not quite," I replied. "But here, use yours to take this stuff outside." I handed him the squashed cardboard and the rest of the garbage. "And make sure you put it in the right bin: Brown or Blue."

"Got it," he said with a wink. "A little blue, brown and green for our red, white and blue."

Published in *Chicken Soup for the Soul Celebrates Grandmothers*

778 words

Make a Memory

by B.J. Taylor

"Are you and the kids going to be home this weekend?" I asked my son. "I want to come up and see you guys."

"We'll be home. When can you get here?"

"I found an affordable flight on the Internet. I'll be there in three days."

"Cool. I'll tell the kids."

"I want to do something fun. Let's make Christmas cookies—the kind we used to make when you were a kid, the cutout ones that you bake and then decorate with icing and colored sugars."

"Yeah. I like those. And the boys will, too."

It would be a messy, fun, memory-filled weekend. Since every moment I spend with my grandchildren is precious, I didn't want to waste time going to the grocery store once I arrived at their house. Nor did I want to bend over a mixing bowl when I could be holding a child in my arms. So, I made the dough and the frosting ahead of time. After mixing up the dough, I placed it in an airtight container. Then I made a butter frosting, licking the bowl and the beaters afterward, just like I did when I was a young mom, raising two sons. Oh, what memories!

After pouring the frosting into another container, and putting both in the fridge, I gathered the colored sugars for decorating. Of course we'd have to have green and red, but how about blue, yellow, pink and purple? It was our tradition, when my boys were small, to add chocolate sprinkles and to use red hots for the tips of the trees and the reindeer noses.

With everything packed and ready, I rolled two suitcases into the airport terminal that Friday morning. The larger one held all the presents to put under the tree, and the other held the rolling pin, cookie cutters, and the dough and frosting containers nestled in ice packs for the trip.

Saturday morning found a house full of kids gathered around the kitchen table. My brother and his children had joined us for the festivities.

"Grandma, can I roll out the dough?" asked nine-year-old Nick.

"I want to make a reindeer," said little five-year-old Cole.

The first few attempts produced Santas that stuck to the floured table and reindeer with only two legs. We kept on going, though, and finally got the hang of it. Some of the kids wanted to throw back the cookies that were misshapen and less than perfect, but we kept every one. It was fun to look back after they were baked to see the elongated star and the funny-looking stocking. After all, it's part of Christmas to accept things just the way they are.

We rolled out the dough many times, and cut out stockings, trees, Santas, reindeer, stars and bells. While we cut out more, we put the first two trays of cookies into the oven. We finished baking the last batch two hours later. We had over four dozen cookies to frost and decorate.

Out came the box from my suitcase with sugars in all shades of the rainbow. We put them in separate bowls, lined up on one side of the table. The adults frosted the cookies and handed them to a waiting child, who would walk along the row of colors and sprinkle a little bit of red, a touch of yellow, and maybe a dash of green.

"I want a stocking, Grandma!" little Cole yelled out.

"I want a star," Amanda demanded. And on it went, the adults barely keeping up with the eager children.

As tray after tray was filled with brightly colored cookies, we oohed and aahed over each one. "Look at mine, Grandma!" shouted Nick. "I put extra frosting on it; see the hump?"

"Look at my bell, Daddy," said Kayla, "it has a Red Hot right at the top."

I thought about the memories we had all just made as I watched my son and his uncle wipe off the table, put all the colored sugar away and grab the vacuum to clean up the floor. Happy memories. Loving memories. Fun times shared with laughter and joy.

"Who made the star with all the different colored points?" "Who made this one with the pretty stripes down the side?" "Nick, is this one yours with the extra frosting on it?" "Can I eat it?"

The afternoon wore into the evening, and cookie after cookie disappeared from the trays. Little hands would reach up and choose just the colors they were looking for. It was a happy day.

But the best part came as music to my ears when I heard, "Grandma, can we do this again next year?"

Published in *Along the Way: Real Life Moments Touched by God*

1235 words

A Boy for Brutus

by B.J. Taylor

"Are you going to take my dog?" the boy asked, his voice quivering. He stood behind his mother with tears in his eyes. I looked away as she scooped him into her arms.

"Remember what I told you, Tommy? We're moving to a small apartment, and we can't take the dog. This nice lady will take him."

"But why?" he wailed.

I tried to control my emotions. I felt bad for Tommy and his mom. The older kids would miss Brutus, she told me, but he was Tommy's dog, so it was toughest for him.

Brutus was a beautiful golden retriever with liquid brown eyes and a coat the color of butterscotch pudding. All he had ever known was this family's love. I couldn't let him go to a shelter where row after row of caged animals paced back and forth, eyes pleading to be rescued from their concrete-and-wire existence.

Listening to Tommy's cries as I walked away with Brutus, I knew I was doing the right thing. So why did it feel so wrong?

Brutus and I settled into a daily routine. Every morning we walked in the neighborhood, and every night I shared popcorn or pieces of a baloney sandwich with him. He often made me laugh as he cocked his head and howled along when I sang.

I was content, but Brutus only seemed truly happy when we met children on our walks. Then his tail wagged, his ears perked up, and his step turned springy. When the kids played fetch with him or wrapped their arms around him, his mouth opened into a smile and his eyes danced. When the children left, his spirit drooped and his eyes clouded with sadness.

One night I sat on the floor with Brutus, I looked into his eyes and felt a connection that seemed beyond words. "I'm not supposed to keep you, am I?" I said aloud. The thought made me sad. I loved this dog. I scratched behind his ears. It would be easy to keep him, but was that the right thing to do?

"I need to find you a home with kids again, where you can chase them around the backyard and play tug-of-war with old socks. You miss resting your head on a boy's tummy when he watches television or curling up by his feet when he does his homework."

Brutus let out a long sigh and stretched out on the floor at my side. I knew I was doing all I could to make him happy. I gave him a home when he desperately needed one. But he needed something I couldn't give. It wasn't fair to keep him to myself without the companionship of kids he so desperately craved.

"Okay, Brutus," I whispered in his ear. "Let's find you a family." He licked my face and wagged his tail.

"God," I prayed, "you always provide just what we need. Please help me." Soon I felt a comfortable peace. Somehow I knew that Brutus was destined to be a young boy's dog again.

A short time later I was walking Brutus when three young girls ran out of a house.

"Your dog is so beautiful," the youngest girl said, kneeling and stroking Brutus' head. "We want a dog just like him!"

I told her I was looking for a home for Brutus. "Do you girls have a brother?"

"No," the girls said.

"Can you wait here while I go get my dad?" asked the youngest. "Please, please?"

I was dumbfounded. This couldn't be right. This family had only daughters. As I waited, the older girls continued to pet Brutus, whose tail continued wagging.

"My dad is busy," the little girl said when she returned, "but can he talk to you later?"

That evening the father came over. "I've wanted a golden retriever for the kids," he said, "but I'm not sure how the girls will adjust to a pet. Can I take Brutus for a week to decide if it will work out?"

At the end of the week, the father walked back up the sidewalk with Brutus on his leash. "I have bad news," he said. "A dog is more responsibility than the girls thought, and they aren't ready for it. I'm sorry, but I have to give Brutus back."

I took Brutus into the house. His eyes were sadder now than before. I needed to find him a home with children and quickly.

I looked at Brutus and silently prayed. *Okay, now what?* That's when the idea came to place an ad in our community paper. While I was at work, my sister would show the dog to any callers. The day after the paper was circulated, my sister called to say a family was on their way to see Brutus, and she would let them in. As the next hour dragged by, I was torn between wanting what was best for Brutus and not wanting to give him up.

Then the phone rang again.

"B.J., the family is here—a mom and dad with their four children. They seem really nice, and they want to take Brutus with them."

"I haven't even said goodbye!" I told her, a little stunned by the suddenness.

"Well, they really like him. What do you want to do?" my sister gently pressed.

"Tell them they can take him, but get their address and phone number," I said. "Tell them I want to come by tomorrow before work to say goodbye."

When I came home that night, I gathered Brutus' extra leash and toys to deliver the next day. My eyes were filled with tears. In the morning, I called the Millers' house at 7:30 sharp. "I hope I didn't wake you."

"With a little baby and youngsters to get ready for school, this is definitely not too early. Come on over," Mrs. Miller said.

On the way, I felt excited. Brutus was with children again! Even though I would miss him, I knew he would be happy. I parked in front of the ranch-style home and walked to the door. Through the kitchen window, I saw a lot of activity—sandwiches being assembled for school lunches, a little girl laughing and eating breakfast, and Mrs. Miller watching a baby in her swing.

"Come on in, B.J.," she invited when I knocked.

"Thank you for letting me come to say goodbye," I said.

"No problem. I understand. Brutus is in the family room with Dan."

We walked down the hall. In the family room I saw well-worn furniture, a television set in the corner, and a pet door leading to a grassy backyard with a swing set and huge trees. A teenage boy knelt next to Brutus.

"Hello, Brutus," I said. He raised his head and wagged his tail. He walked to me and I petted his silky coat. I looked for the sadness that used to be in those liquid brown eyes, but now I only saw contentment.

"This is our son, Dan," Mrs. Miller said. "Dan is a big help to me with the younger children, and he's always doing helpful chores for the neighbors. We decided that Brutus will be Dan's dog. We've always wanted a golden retriever," she added.

I had only been a stepping-stone in this dog's journey through life. Now Brutus had a family again and, best of all, a boy of his very own.

Published in *Guideposts* May 2006

935 words

Crash!

My computer was my lifeline. Had it become a trap?

by B.J. Taylor

Clunk...claaack...cachunk! What was that noise? I was saving a file, like I did every day—dozens of times a day. My PC had its little idio-syncrasies, but it had never made a noise like this before. "Okay, computer, don't mess with me." I highlighted the item again and punched "Enter." *Carunk!* My screen dissolved ominously into darkness. I rebooted. Nothing. I tried again. No luck. Panic crept over me. I *can't live without my computer,* I thought.

Frantically I fumbled through some papers on my desk, looking for the phone number of the computer guy. *Don't tell me it's on my hard drive,* I thought. Along with every other important phone number and address.

Like a lot of folks these days, my computer is my life. First thing in the morning, I turn it on. I check the news, the weather, traffic—you name it. I e-mail my friends and shop online. I save our family photos. And I track all the financials for my home-based business on my computer. It's efficient, practical and, at times, all-consuming. I even eat my lunch at the keyboard most days.

Finally I found the computer guy's business card and urgently dialed his number. "Bill, I said, "something's gone terribly wrong. I was just saving a document and the computer made this awful nose. Now it won't start up."

"Sounds like your hard drive," he said. "Did you back everything up on discs like I told you?"

I cringed. "I saved some stuff," I said. But how long ago? And how much?

"I'll come over, but I'm afraid that anything that's on the hard drive is lost."

I hung up the phone in a daze. *Lost!* All my company data. The photos of the grandkids—gone. Links to my favorite web sites, my address book—gone, gone, gone. "It's just a machine," I tried to tell myself. Machines break down. Sometimes they need to be replaced. It's not the end of the world.

But it felt like the end of the world. My whole life was wrapped up in that box of metal and plastic with its megabytes of storage. Even my spiritual life. I kept up with my friends and their prayer requests online. *God*, I sighed, staring at the blank screen, *this is bad.*

I paced around the house until Bill arrived, then watched him take the cover off the CPU and reveal the inner mysteries of the machine. Huh. Nothing more than wires, metal and plastic. How could it have taken over my life?

"Yep," he said briskly after tinkering around, "it's your hard drive, all right. Shot. It can be replaced, but we'll have to reload your programs and data." He packed up the computer, leaving the monitor with me, and was gone.

Suddenly my days seemed empty. I walked by the darkened screen, wishing it would magically come to life. I'd think of a web site I needed to visit, a present I wanted to order, or a friend I owed an e-mail. Backup discs? I hadn't backed anything up in two years. Why bother? Computers take care of everything. Can't they back themselves up? I tried reconstructing my business accounts on a legal paid, but it was no use. I needed a computer keyboard to think.

I ate my lunch at the dining room table that first full day without my PC. Oh, how I longed to see that mail icon pop up. Instead I looked out at the hummingbirds darting around the sycamore tree. That afternoon I sat on the sofa and read. Nice to read something that wasn't on a screen, easier on the eyes. There is something so *physical* about reading real type on paper, as if the eyes have an almost tactile relationship to the words. But then my mind would snap back: If *only* I *hadn't lost all my files. What am* I *going to do?*

I told all my friends whose phone numbers I could remember about my disaster. One called me back. "You know, B.J., I was thinking of what happened to all the photos you lost…well, you sent a lot of them to me. Want me to send digital copies to you?"

"That'd be great. As soon as my computer is back."

Now, what about my company data? Full of misgivings, I called up my accountant. "I've had this terrible crisis with my computer and I've lost everything on my hard drive," I said.

"I have all your tax information from the past few years," he told me. "I can download it and send it to you. Then you can use it to set up your files when your computer is back up."

"B.J.," another friend called. "I know you're worried about getting everybody's e-mail addresses again, but I'll send you the ones I have. They're all people you know."

I returned to my view of the sycamore tree and the birds. Maybe this wasn't going to be so bad. *Lord,* I thought, *maybe you're trying to tell me something. It's not the computer that's so important, it's the people it connects me to.*

Bill returned with my new hard drive—in three days, not the week I had feared. The computer came back up with its cute little arpeggio. "Thanks for your help," I e-mailed my friends. Then I logged on to my favorite spiritual web site and posted a prayer. "I thank God my computer is up and running again," I wrote. "But most of all I thank God for all the people who are still there even when my hard drive isn't!"

Published in *Chicken Soup for the Soul: Divorce and Recovery*

821 words

Tick Tock

by B.J. Taylor

There it stood on the front lawn. Tall, stately, mahogany wood and glass. Three brass weights hung from long chains. A brass sun and moon rose and fell across shiny numerals.

My grandfather clock. My prize. My possession. Set out on the green grass like a discarded bath towel.

It was appropriate that this timepiece marked the end of our marriage. We'd sure spent enough years trying to make it work—seventeen. There are all kinds of reasons for two people to stay together, and all kinds of reasons for them to move apart. It was time for us to move apart. And that was harder than I had expected.

"I'd like to have the grandfather clock," I had said to my ex-husband on the telephone.

"Forget it. It's part of the house and it stays."

He lived in the house now and I was leaving the state. I had wanted to take the clock with me. After all, I had worked hard for it.

I sold Tupperware at home parties for quite some time, and one day they announced a contest. "You earn points for every sale you make," the owner of the distributorship announced. "Here's a full-color catalog. Find something you want to have. There's everything from microwave ovens to vacuum cleaners and toasters." I opened the glossy brochure and flipped through the pages. My eyes stopped on a photo of a regal clock. I never had anything so beautiful, so elegant. I could hear the three different chimes, the melodies ringing on every quarter, half and full hour. I had to have it.

When I reached my goal, the owner handed me an order form to fill out. My hands shook with joy. I bypassed the blender and the dishwasher and checked the box for the grandfather clock. It was delivered a couple of months later and we set it up in the dining room. That's where it sat for years.

Now, although just a piece of furniture to my ex, the clock remained a symbol of achievement and success to me.

"Come on," I pleaded, "you don't care about it. Let me have it."

"No," was his clipped reply.

I hung up. He was stubborn. There was no way that clock would be mine.

A few days later, I drove down my old street. There stood the clock on the front lawn where all the neighbors could see it. A glaring symbol of the end of our marriage. The end of our time together. I screeched to a stop and turned into the driveway. I walked up to the door and knocked. He answered from inside. "Take it," he said.

"What?" I didn't think I heard right.

"You can have it."

I swallowed hard. "Thanks," I mumbled, and then turned from the doorway. I wanted to ask why he threw it out on the lawn like a bone for a dog, but I held my tongue. There it stood, and it was mine. I didn't question his second thoughts.

Luckily I had a station wagon. I unhooked the weights and the pendulum and placed them on the front seat. The clock was tall and awkward, but surprisingly light. I'm sure he saw me struggle with it. I gently lowered the top and dragged it across the grass to the rear of the car. I set the top end inside the tailgate and then lifted the bottom. Nudging it forward on the carpeting, I pushed it up to just behind the front seats. I couldn't get the tailgate closed, but it didn't matter—I didn't have far to go.

I jumped into the driver's seat and slowly backed out of the gravel driveway. When I got to my dad's house a few blocks away, I unloaded the clock into the garage. I shimmied it over to the wall and covered it with a large blanket. That's where it sat until a moving truck came to take me to my new home, my new beginning, my new life.

When I look at the clock now in my new living room, chiming those Westminster melodies on the hour, I am reminded of the times of my life. I don't regret my first marriage. I don't regret my divorce. Life is sweeter because of all that I have experienced. I appreciate each movement of the minute hand, each turn of the hour. The days melt one into another, and the clock doesn't stop.

But it did that day when my ex took a step in the right direction. After all, we had spent what felt like a lifetime together. We were two young kids married too soon, but we had many wonderful times together. Not one moment of our marriage was wasted. Each minute was the way it was meant to be. Each hour a blessing. We learned a lot about ourselves, about our loves, about our lives.

Life changes.

Tick tock.

Published in *Chicken Soup for the Tea Lovers Soul*

740 words

Sweet Dreams

by B.J. Taylor

"Why does he always have big projects on a Friday afternoon?" I wailed when I walked in the door after work.

"What's the matter, Dear?" my mother-in-law said from the kitchen.

I threw my purse onto the counter. "Oh, my boss. He had me work late again. I didn't get out of the office until six o'clock. Now here it is almost seven. Why does he do that before the weekend?" I walked over to the refrigerator and opened it.

"Don't worry about dinner. I made lasagna," she said.

"Oh, that was nice of you. Let's chop up a salad to go with it." I pulled out the lettuce, cucumber and tomatoes. We shared a cutting board, and chopped and sliced together, filling our bowls.

The lasagna came out of the oven hot and bubbly. It was delicious, but my mind swirled with thoughts of all the work waiting for me on my desk Monday morning. I was still miffed at my boss. We rinsed off the dinner dishes and put them into the dishwasher. My husband was on a three-day business trip, and this was the first night of my mother-in-law's visit. She'd be spending a few weeks with us before returning home.

"I'm sorry I came home in such a crabby mood. I didn't mean to take it out on you," I said.

"Don't worry about me. I can handle it. It's you I worry about. You shouldn't get so upset over work."

"I can't help it. My boss drives me crazy!"

"There were bosses like that in my day, too. There's only one way to deal with them," she said.

I was all ears, ready to hear the words of wisdom on how to put my boss in his place, how to tell him not to give me an overabundance of work, how to make him appreciate all that I do for him. "What's the secret?" I asked.

"A cup of tea."

"Tea? How can that help?"

"Let me show you. Sit down here on the sofa," she said as she patted the end.

I did as she directed. I sank into the soft pillow back and kicked off my shoes.

"Now close your eyes and relax. I'll be back in a few minutes."

I could hear her footsteps on the tile and knew she was in the kitchen. I listened as the cupboard door creaked when she took cups out. The water ran in the sink. Then I heard the ping ping ping of the burner lighting on the gas stove. Minutes later, the kettle whistled.

"Okay, open your eyes," she said.

She stood in front of me with two steaming mugs. Dangling out the side of each was a string with a square piece of paper at the end.

"Here," she said as she handed me one of the mugs.

I took it with both hands. It wasn't too hot, just nice and warm. "Thanks," I said.

"Don't thank me yet. Sit and enjoy."

She joined me on the sofa and we sat with our cups in our hands. I took a sip. It was good. "What kind is this?" I asked.

"It's a favorite of mine. I bring it with me wherever I go."

I felt myself relax as I sipped the tea, warmth flooding through not just my fingers and hands, but through my whole being. I felt calmer.

"So this tea—it makes bosses go away?" I asked, smiling.

She laughed. "No, nothing will do that. But it will make you forget about it for a little while."

We sat, drank, and enjoyed each other's company. We talked about some of the things we wanted to do while she was visiting. Time flew by. Soon, we were both down to the last drops in our cups. I got up and took the mugs to the kitchen sink.

"That was really good," I said, then covered my mouth as I yawned. "I'm ready to put my pajamas on and go to bed."

"Me, too," she replied.

"How about tomorrow night we watch a movie after dinner?" I said.

"Sounds great. I'll even make you another cup of tea." She began climbing the stairs to the guest room. "Good night. See you in the morning."

"By the way. What was the name of that tea?" I asked.

She stopped halfway up the steps, turned her head toward me and smiled. "Sweet Dreams," she said.

Want more stories to study? *Sunny Side Up: Inspirational Stories for Tough Times, Women, Dog & Cat Lovers* is loaded with personal experience, true life stories.

Finding The Formula
In The Study Guide Stories

As you studied each of the stories, you determined how **P MS** TO A **T** played out in each of them. Did the story start with a captivating hook? What was the story problem? How many scenes were there? Where did the turnaround occur? Did it have a satisfying takeaway?

The answers are below.

Blue, Brown & Green for Our Red, White & Blue

<u>Opening Hook:</u>

> "You've got to be kidding," I raged. "I'm not going to separate our trash into three different containers. Forget it."
>
> "It says here we'll be fined if we don't," my husband countered.
>
> "Well, I'm not going to," I stubbornly replied.

<u>Problem:</u> I didn't want to sort the trash as stated in this next paragraph:

> Chicken bones, potato peelings, cardboard cartons, plastic milk jugs; I put all of it together in one bag into one trashcan every night. That's the way I'd always done it, and that's the way I wanted to keep doing it. None of this fancy-schmancy sorting for me.

<u>Multiple Scenes:</u>

The first scene is the behemoth trucks lumbering down the street and depositing the trash bins.

The second scene is juggling the gardening supplies, the dog house, and the wire shelving unit to make room for Big Blue, Big Green, and Big Brown.

The third scene is the dialog about what items go in what trash bin.

The fourth scene is in the kitchen when I'm smashing the cardboard carton, again using dialog to show the scene.

Turnaround:

"You, sorting trash?"

"Yes, and don't be so shocked. It doesn't take as much time as I thought."

"What happened to fussing about three separate containers?"

"I don't know. I guess I hated change. But now that I'm used to it, I love doing my part."

Takeaway: I say "doing my part" but don't overdo it by adding "for the environment." Do you get the feeling, though, that they are helping the environment by the paragraphs at the end of the story? That's the takeaway, in a subtle, uplifting, feel-good way.

"That's my girl," my husband said, when he took me in his arms and hugged me. "And look at those muscles you're getting. Almost as big as mine."

"Not quite," I replied. "But here, use yours to take this stuff outside." I handed him the squashed cardboard and the rest of the garbage. "And make sure you put it in the right bin: Brown or Blue."

"Got it," he said with a wink. "A little blue, brown and green for our red, white and blue."

Make a Memory

Opening Hook: Not the most captivating opening hook, but it is dialog and it at least entices the reader to keep reading.

> "Are you and the kids going to be home this weekend?" I asked my son. "I want to come up and see you guys."
> "We'll be home. When can you get here?"

Problem: The story problem appears first when I want to spend time with my son and grandchildren, then the problem becomes one of not wanting to waste time going to the grocery store, but wanting to be with and hold those grandchildren in my arms, which is an extension of the main problem. Both are indicated here from the story:

> "Are you and the kids going to be home this weekend?" I asked my son. "I want to come up and see you guys."
> … Since every moment I spend with my grandchildren is precious, I didn't want to waste time going to the grocery store once I arrived at their house. Nor did I want to bend over a mixing bowl when I could be holding a child in my arms.

Multiple Scenes:

The first scene is when I'm mixing up the dough, the butter frosting, licking the beaters, and gathering the colored sugars.

The second scene is at the house with all the kids and family, with dialog from Nick and Cole, rolling the dough and cutting out cookies.

The third scene is the table filled with bowls of rainbow colors of sugar as the adults frost the cookies and the kids decorate them. More dialog with the children.

This is a short story of only 778 words, so there are only the three scenes.

Turnaround: I had been missing my son and grandchildren. The turnaround occurs when I think about the happy memories we have made.

As tray after tray was filled with brightly colored cookies, we oohed and aahed over each one. "Look at mine, Grandma!" shouted Nick. "I put extra frosting on it; see the hump?"

"Look at my bell, Daddy," said Kayla, "it has a Red Hot right at the top."

I thought about the memories we had all just made as I watched my son and his uncle wipe off the table, put all the colored sugar away and grab the vacuum to clean up the floor. Happy memories. Loving memories. Fun times shared with laughter and joy.

Takeaway: No need to beat the reader over the head that it is crucial to spend time with the family, with the growing children. The reader knows these moments are important.

Give them a feel-good ending with the subtle bit of dialog from one of the children. They will get it, as indicated in this final paragraph of the story:

> The afternoon wore into the evening, and cookie after cookie disappeared from the trays. Little hands would reach up and choose just the colors they were looking for. It was a happy day. But the best part came as music to my ears when I heard, "Grandma, can we do this again next year?"

A Boy for Brutus

Opening Hook:

> "Are you going to take my dog?" the boy asked, his voice quivering. He stood behind his mother with tears in his eyes. I looked away as she scooped him into her arms.
>
> "Remember what I told you, Tommy? We're moving to a small apartment, and we can't take the dog. This nice lady will take him."
>
> "But why?" he wailed.

Problem: The story problem is this dog needs a home, which comes up right away in the opening hook. I step in to help the family. At that point, you might think the story is over, right? The dog has a home. But you find out I have unsettled feelings, which keeps the reader engaged:

Brutus was a beautiful golden retriever with liquid brown eyes and a coat the color of butterscotch pudding. All he had ever known was this family's love. I couldn't let him go to a shelter where row after row of caged animals paced back and forth, eyes pleading to be rescued from their concrete-and-wire existence.

Listening to Tommy's cries as I walked away with Brutus. I knew I was doing the right thing. So why did it feel so wrong?

Multiple Scenes:

The first scene is when I sit on the floor with Brutus and look into his eyes. This is played out with dialog that includes a long sigh from the dog, a whisper into the dog's ear, and a prayer to God for help in finding him a home.

The second scene is the walk with Brutus where I meet three young girls. Dialog moves the story forward as the girls' father comes over, takes the dog, and then brings him back.

The third scene occurs after an ad is placed in the paper and a family wants to take Brutus. Dialog again brings the reader right into the feelings I have as I realize it is time to let Brutus go.

The fourth scene is at the new house with the family when I pet Brutus one last time.

Turnaround: A turnaround moment comes before the fourth scene, and then is felt even stronger during that fourth scene when I see contentment in the dog's eyes. I'll show you both places in the story here:

> On the way, I felt excited. Brutus was with children again! Even though I would miss him, I knew he would be happy.

And here…

> "Hello, Brutus," I said. He raised his head and wagged his tail. He walked to me and I petted his silky coat. I looked for the sadness that used to be in those liquid brown eyes, but now I only saw contentment.

Takeaway: Subtle, feel-good ending:

> I had only been a stepping-stone in this dog's journey through life. Now Brutus had a family again and, best of all, a boy of his very own.

Crash!

Opening Hook:

> Clunk…claaack…cachunk! What was that noise? I was saving a file, like I did every day—dozens of times a day. My PC had its little idiosyncrasies, but

it had never made a noise like this before. "Okay, computer, don't mess with me." I highlighted the item again and punched "Enter." *Carunk!*

<u>Problem</u>:

My screen dissolved ominously into darkness. I rebooted. Nothing. I tried again. No luck. Panic crept over me. I *can't live without my computer*, I thought.

<u>Multiple Scenes</u>:

The first scene is the phone call I make to the computer tech and the dialog between us.

The second scene is when the computer tech arrives and takes the cover off the computer, revealing the inner workings of the machine, and the dialog about the hard drive.

The third scene is when I eat lunch at the dining room table, watch the hummingbirds, sit on the sofa and read a book.

The fourth scene is the dialog with friends and my accountant, who help me with everything lost on the computer.

<u>Turnaround</u>: I turn around from thinking I can't live without my computer to finding out there is joy in my friends, the birds, and even the trees.

I returned to my view of the sycamore tree and the birds. Maybe this wasn't going to be so bad. *Lord,* I thought, *maybe you're trying to tell me something. It's not the computer that's so important, it's the people it connects me to.*

<u>Takeaway</u>: It would be easy to lapse into a heavy-handed message about the need to back up a computer, and even to give recommendations for how to do that. But that's not the point of an inspirational story, and not what we need in a feel-good takeaway. Do you feel the subtle ending helps the reader to see there is more to life than a computer?

Bill returned with my new hard drive—in three days, not the week I had feared. The computer came back up with its cute little arpeggio. "Thanks for your help," I e-mailed my friends. Then I logged on to my favorite spiritual web site and posted a prayer. "I thank God my computer is up and running again," I wrote. "But most of all I thank God for all the people who are still there even when my hard drive isn't!"

Tick Tock

<u>Opening Hook</u>: I didn't use dialog in this opening, but the statements in short, punchy, weighted words hook the reader into wanting to know what is going on and why:

There it stood on the front lawn. Tall, stately, mahogany wood and glass. Three brass weights hung from long chains. A brass sun and moon rose and fell across shiny numerals.

My grandfather clock. My prize. My possession. Set out on the green grass like a discarded bath towel.

Problem: I want the grandfather clock, but my ex is stubborn and won't give in. I'm angry with him and will have to accept the clock will no longer be mine. Notice I did not go into detail about why we are divorcing. There are many reasons couples move apart, and each couple will have their own set of circumstances. The general statements work, and keep the reader interested in the story about the grandfather clock and whether my ex and I work it out, and not the history behind the divorce.

… There are all kinds of reasons for two people to stay together, and all kinds of reasons for them to move apart. It was time for us to move apart. And that was harder than I had expected.

"I'd like to have the grandfather clock," I had said to my ex-husband on the telephone.

"Forget it. It's part of the house and it stays."

Multiple Scenes:

The first scene shows how I came to earn the clock. Dialog with the owner of the distributorship keeps the reader engaged.

The second scene is when I drive down my old street and see the clock on the front lawn. I walk up to the door of the house and my ex tells me, "Take it."

The third scene is dragging the clock to the station wagon, nudging it forward inside, and then taking it to my dad's garage.

This story is 821 words. I did not need a fourth scene.

Turnaround: I turn around from being angry with my ex to realizing we were two people who were once in love. Time doesn't erase the past.

> When I look at the clock now in my new living room, chiming those Westminster melodies on the hour, I am reminded of the times of my life. I don't regret my first marriage. I don't regret my divorce. Life is sweeter because of all that I have experienced. I appreciate each movement of the minute hand, each turn of the hour. The days melt one into another, and the clock doesn't stop.

Takeaway: A feel-good, subtle takeaway about each day, each moment, a blessing.

> But it did that day when my ex took a step in the right direction. After all, we had spent what felt like a lifetime together. We were two young kids married too soon, but we had many wonderful times together. Not one moment of our marriage was wasted. Each minute was the way it was meant

to be. Each hour a blessing. We learned a lot about ourselves, about our loves, about our lives.

Life changes.

Tick tock.

Sweet Dreams

<u>Opening Hook</u>:

"Why does he always have big projects on a Friday afternoon?" I wailed when I walked in the door after work.

"What's the matter, Dear?" my mother-in-law said from the kitchen.

I threw my purse onto the counter. "Oh, my boss. He had me work late again." ...

<u>Problem</u>: In this story of only 740 words, the opening hook also serves as the problem. I'm angry with my boss.

... I didn't get out of the office until six o'clock. Now here it is almost seven. Why does he do that before the weekend?"

<u>Multiple Scenes</u>:

The first scene is the dialog with my mother-in-law where I apologize for coming home in a crabby mood. She tells me there is only one way to deal with bosses like that.

The second scene shows my mother-in-law making tea in the kitchen, the sounds of the cupboard door creaking, the water running in the sink, and the burner lighting on the stove.

The third scene is my mother-in-law with two cups of steaming tea. She hands one to me and I put both hands around the warm mug.

Turnaround: I turn around from being angry at my boss to understanding I can handle it today by forgetting about it for a little while.

> I felt myself relax as I sipped the tea, warmth flooding through not just my fingers and hands, but through my whole being. I felt calmer.
> "So this tea—it makes bosses go away?" I asked, smiling.
> She laughed. "No, nothing will do that. But it will make you forget about it for a little while."

Takeaway: A subtle, feel-good ending. Do you feel it in the final line? Without relaxing, without taking a moment to "forget about it for a little while," I doubt I would have had sweet dreams that night.

> … She began climbing the stairs to the guest room. "Good night. See you in the morning."
> "By the way. What was the name of that tea?" I asked.

She stopped halfway up the steps, turned her head toward me and smiled. "Sweet Dreams," she said.

ACKNOWLEDGMENTS

I'd like to thank the many writers who encouraged me to write this book. You have attended my workshop classes, signed up for my Taylor's Tips Newsletter, and received my blog posts. I am in awe of your inspiration. You motivate me to do more.

Thanks also to the numerous people who have been my instructors, from whom I have learned a great deal, the conference directors who selected me to speak at their events, and the friends on social media who have shared a wealth of knowledge over the years. I couldn't have accomplished so much without your support.

To you, personally. My valued reader. Without putting the multitude of names on paper, my acknowledgements encompass the entire 20-plus years I have been a writer. *Thank you for sharing your world with me.*

ALSO BY B.J. TAYLOR

Charlie Bear: What a Headstrong Rescue Dog Taught Me about Life, Love, and Second Chances

Sunny Side Up: Inspiring Stories for Tough Times, Women, Dog & Cat Lovers

The Complete Guide to Writers Groups That Work

20861446R00086

Made in the USA
San Bernardino, CA
27 April 2015